6.15

THE CARE AND REPAIR
OF BOOKS

THE CARE
AND REPAIR
OF BOOKS

by Harry Miller Lydenberg
and John Archer

Revised
by John Alden

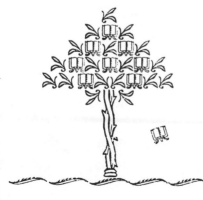

NEW YORK 1960

R. R. BOWKER COMPANY

Library of Congress Card Catalog No. 60-11980

Copyright © 1931, 1945, 1960 by R. R. Bowker Company

62 West 45th Street, New York 36, N. Y.

Price $6.15

FOURTH REVISED EDITION
SECOND PRINTING

Printed in the United States of America

Contents

Introduction

FOR MANY of us occupied with books and their care it comes as a surprise to learn how recent the scientific approach to their preservation and restoration is. Not that the problems in question have been viewed in the past with indifference, and that remedies have not been advanced. In the field of repair the extraordinary skill of binders and penmen in reconstructing damaged books compels admiration; and the affection and effort lavished upon books as physical objects still find an echoing response.

The fact remains that many earlier methods were largely pragmatic, and based upon an imperfect understanding of the nature of books. Only in the past sixty years have serious attempts been made at really basic research in the field, to understand why books, and the materials used in their repair, behave in the way they do.

One of the pleasures of preparing the present edition of Messrs. Lydenberg and Archer's pioneer work is that it is now possible to pay particular tribute to the part which Mr. Lydenberg has played in the research done in America. For it was at his initiative that, in 1929, a study of the effect of city air on books stored under the usual library conditions was recommended by the American Library Association, of which he was then president. With a grant provided by the Carnegie Corporation, the National Research Council established fellowships at the National Bureau of Standards to undertake this and related investigations. Later this grant was supplemented by others included in the regular funds for the Bureau appropriated by Congress.

Although the depression put an end to the funds available, the results of the studies are incorporated in the *Summary Report of the Bureau of Standards Research on Preservation of Records*, prepared by A. E. Kimberly and B. W. Scribner (Bureau of Standards Miscellaneous Publication No. 144), issued in 1934. It stands as a milestone in American preservation studies, and as a monument to Mr. Lydenberg's recognition of a major problem in American librarianship.

In this Mr. Lydenberg found himself one with a widespread movement which may be said to date from 1898. At an international conference of librarians held at the Monastery of Saint Gall in 1898, the then prefect of the Vatican Library, later cardinal, Franz Ehrle, had called for a reappraisal of existing restoration methods. Similarly in 1900 the Society for the Encouragement of Arts, Manufacture, and Commerce, in England, set up a committee for study of the deterioration of book leathers. Following the First World War a research laboratory was instituted at the British Museum to deal with its preservation problems, and the results both in basic research and in methods advocated have been universally influential. Somewhat later Alfonso Gallo founded at Rome his Istituto di Patologia del Libro (Institute for the Pathology of the Book), where comprehensive investigations relating to the book as artifact have been undertaken. To meet their particular problems, so closely allied to those of bookmen, archivists have also been active. In this the National Archives of the United States has been a leader, but mention must also be made of the theoretical and practical work carried on by the National Archives of India, under its able preservation officer, Dr. R. C. Gupta, especially in terms of tropical climates.

More recently UNESCO has established at Rome an International Center for the Study of the Preservation and Restoral of Cultural Property. Included in its areas of interest are not solely museum objects but books and manuscripts as well. With H. J. Plenderleith, till recently chief of the British Museum's Research Laboratory, as its director, the Center promises to be a valuable clearinghouse for preservation matters throughout the world.

As a result of such efforts by institutions and individuals we can today approach the care and repair of books with greater confidence, with a richer measure of hope that in our methods we may not do more harm than good, and with assurance that though problems continue to arise the means for their solution may well be found.

In their earlier editions of this work Messrs. Lydenberg and Archer limited themselves to meeting conditions prevailing in the temperate zone of the western world, while recognizing that the measures suggested might well be adapted to other climates. There can be little doubt that, regardless of climate, the principles of preservation and repair are indeed universal, and if one grasps them one is prepared to find solutions for local situations. The difficulties which arise are often a matter of degree rather than of kind.

What is perhaps more difficult is to reconcile the varying objectives of preservation. These derive from the disparate demands made upon the book itself. For some a book is not only a text but also in itself an object of interest. For others the text alone is significant. The latter are not going to care much—apart from convenience—how the text is preserved. Those charged with the preservation of books and manuscripts must ask themselves what objectives they serve in their particular circumstances—and not be unduly influenced by the objectives of others. The antiquarian bookseller, the administrator of the rare book collection, the public librarian, each will have his or her own aim in view. It may be the handsome, richly gilt, morocco-bound volume of Dickens, or the shabby but original binding of an incunable (preserved in a modern case), or the plastic-jacketed, clean, and inviting contemporary novel. On occasion economic necessity may demand expedients, yet there will be other times when the importance of the materials to be protected transcends financial measurements.

In preparing this new edition of a work whose usefulness

has been so amply manifested, an effort has been made to retain its established virtues, and to supplement them with reports on developments in preservation in recent years of which the library administrator and the technician should be aware. No attempt has been made, however, to present all possible methods and practices: the stress has been made upon those which seem likely to be most widely available and practicable, those which can be carried out by the individual or librarian without recourse to exceptional skill or machinery. For those who wish to pursue their problems further, it is hoped that the List of References given in Chapter 9 will provide the necessary guide.

J.A.

Chapter One

THE CARE OF BOOKS
IN GENERAL

Books are like children in more ways than one: in their response to care and attention in early life, for one thing, and in their response to heredity and environment for another. It was the Autocrat of the Breakfast-Table, was it not, whose first specification for his "man of family" demanded "four or five generations of gentlemen and gentlewomen"? For our "book of family" the same four or five generations of gentle forebears are equally necessary. The book's early life will be happier, its maturity longer, its final disappearance more distant if, like a child, it has found its lines cast among kindly and sympathetic friends and parents. Hygienic living conditions, proper prophylaxis, prevention of disease are more important than medication or drugs, while thoughtful and skillful attention by competent, well-trained, experienced physicians and surgeons is essential when need arises.

The child has better assurance of long and useful life if he has been properly clad, has received proper food and attention, has found his lot among people who will care for him and free him from unfair demands on his strength. The book has better assurance of long and useful life if it was brought into the world on paper of lasting quality, paper fitted to the needs the volume must serve, the demands it must meet. It will have better assurance of long and useful life if it is clad in protecting garments selected with judgment, cut and fitted with skill, if it is certain of proper food at proper times in proper amounts, is brought to appreciative hands as soon as indications of weakness begin to show themselves, treated with proper care and attention when major operations are called for, and housed under conditions most beneficial for such companions, helpmates, friends.

For most of us the book is more like an adopted child than one of our own flesh and blood, since it usually reaches us full grown and mature. Our control over its youth and adolescence is usually slight. Happy the man permitted to stand by and help to give shape and form to the child of his brain, to select type and paper, to choose boards and cover stock and end papers, to decide color and weight of cloth or leather, to sketch the lettering and decoration in this form or that. On the other hand, it is perhaps unduly captious to criticize the publishers of the books when they do not incorporate in them those qualities which will ensure their well-being beyond the immediate needs which the publishers serve, those of a public which buys most of our books and will no doubt be satisfied if they last a human lifetime. We who think in terms not of a generation but of centuries have taken upon ourselves a peculiar responsibility, but it is also a rewarding one, as we take up the challenge offered.

With most of us the book must be housed under conditions over which we have less control than over many other more material things that enter into our daily lives. Our books are kept in buildings as warm or as cool during the heating season as our wishes or financial means permit. During the summer the rooms are hot or cool, dry or damp, suffer harm or rejoice in favoring conditions that depend on the weather and are happily independent of our control.

AIR CONDITIONING. Fortunately the development of air conditioning does give us some means of coping with environment, both for ourselves and for our books, and what was once viewed as a luxury and a concession to human frailty is increasingly recognized as a necessity for the well-being both of human beings and of the books and manuscripts which we seek to preserve. As will be stated again and again in the pages which follow, the prevention of deterioration is far more important than skill in repair. And in attempting to forestall damage, air conditioning is the most effective means, controlling as it does both chemical and biological enemies of books.

What was a comparatively new aspect of library administration when earlier editions of this work appeared has now been accepted as indispensable for the library seeking to promote the greatest possible longevity of its books. Moreover, what was once envisaged simply in terms of the control of temperature has been enlarged to that of humidity and the purity of the air as well.

For books the ideal temperature is one of from 65 to 70 degrees, and the ideal relative humidity between 50 and 60 per cent, accompanied by the complete washing and filtering of air to remove noxious gases at all temperatures and all humidities. Not only must air taken from external sources be cleaned, but filters must also be provided to control the introduction of oil from the air-conditioning machinery itself, and to absorb the dust introduced by books or clothing within the building. It is essential, furthermore, that air conditioning be provided on a twenty-four-hour basis at all seasons of the year. For the expansion and contraction of materials through variation in heat and moisture will with the passage of time weaken them—a form of paper or of leather fatigue not incomparable with metal fatigue—howsoever imperceptibly this may occur.

That air conditioning is expensive cannot be denied. On the other hand we should bear in mind that there are books whose intellectual or emotional value ought not to be appraised in monetary terms. In economic terms we may, however, measure against air conditioning the cost of inadequate expedients employed in its absence: the cost of labor for dusting (which may do as much harm as good) or for the more frequent oiling of bindings, or the cost of rebinding itself. Nor should we forget that as more and more libraries install air conditioning for their books, it is to them that potential benefactors look as worthy recipients of their valuable collections.

Many a library will segregate those books whose physical preservation is essential, those books which are not "expendable," and provide for them air-conditioned quarters and the special attention consonant with their importance. That such segregated books are likely to constitute a rare book collection should not frighten the administrator.

Admittedly, in tropical and semitropical climates air conditioning provides problems beyond those of cost. The physical shock for the human being who goes from a room or building where the temperature is maintained at 70 degrees (or, as at the National Archives in Washington, in summer at 80 degrees) into the temperatures of 120 degrees or more experienced in, say, New Delhi, is a real one, and satisfactory solutions for this problem have yet to be evolved. It may lie in air-conditioning the bookstacks alone, while the reading rooms and staff quarters are maintained at an internal temperature less remote from that outside.

CONTACT. And as a parent, or even a stepparent, worries about the company the children entrusted to him are in it must be borne in mind that books can be damaged by almost anything with which they come in contact.

Thus otherwise stable papers can be damaged by contact with acidic papers, such as flyleaves or even bookmarks, or by materials such as celluloid, mistakenly intended to protect. As noted by Barrow, the migration of acids and acidity is an all-too-common phenomenon. Even photostatic replacements of missing leaves are not without their hazards, since the residual acids of developing fluids may damage adjoining pages. Wood pulp newspaper clippings, paper clips, and rubber bands may also be added to the list of unsuitable company for books.

In the following pages an attempt is made to tell about some of these harmful influences that alter the character or shorten the life of books, and to suggest some remedies for cases that appeal for help, to plead for some of the care and attention for these mute but eloquent children of our brains that is given to the children of our loins, to mitigate, if not remove entirely, the iniquities of the fathers visited upon books.

Although various suggestions are here set down for the care and repair of books, manuscripts, broadsides, pamphlets, and other forms of the printed or written message, no doubt other good methods are available. The mere fact of omission here is certainly no reason why they should not be tried, and in an age when constant experimentation and investigation are being carried out, the preservationist will be alert to further developments in the field. Moreover one workman will occasionally succeed with materials and methods that spell failure for his brother at the bench beside him. The real test comes with repeated trials and consistent success.

Chapter Two

THE CARE OF BOOKS
IN THE LIBRARY

Let us suppose you have your books safely delivered new and fresh for current publications, in "good second-hand condition" for the older works, all well printed in a good face of type impressed on good paper, all protected by boards properly sewn in and properly covered with first-class cloth or well-tanned leather, all the work of competent artisans anxious to show the skill of their hands—a set of assumptions probably contrary to fact in many cases but well enough to start with as a preliminary survey.

OPENING THE BOOK. First comes opening the book. Well, opening books is nothing more than opening books, is it not? Nay, not so. Much harm has been done to innocent volumes by careless or thoughtless or ignorant or indifferent handling when opening them. Your reader who really cares for books will put the volume on a table, the back down and the fore edges up, will open the front cover, then the back, will open a few pages next from the back and the front alternately, pressing firmly but gently along the inner margins of the pages, thus lessening the danger of breaking the binding between the sections. If the book has been properly bound all this care may perhaps not be necessary, and modern adhesives do reduce the perils in question. But the danger is that careless or improper binding may be so covered up that harm is done before it is discovered. Whether well bound or poorly bound, there is not the slightest doubt as to the gratitude for careful and appreciative opening felt by the spirit treasured up within these covers.

COLLATING. After the book is opened comes collating, not so portentous or imposing a task as the phrase may perhaps suggest. It means merely making certain that the volume is complete and perfect, usually entailing nothing more than running through the pages one by one to see that all are there and to catch omissions and imperfections. If maps or plates are listed outside the pagination they must be checked for completeness and for proper placing. In early printed books careful checking of signatures and catchwords may be necessary, though this responsibility may be left for the cataloguer, who will wish to do it anyway. This is also the time to see if the cover is damaged, if the corners are bent or broken or battered, if the lining is loose. New books go back to the dealer or publisher if not satisfactory; with old ones decision as to return or repair will depend on circumstances.

CATALOG, ACCESSION, OWNERSHIP RECORDS. Recording and accessioning and cataloguing offer the next hazard. In some private libraries these processes take place in the brain of the owner; in larger collections they become more complicated and more harmful. Some record should certainly be made as to date of receipt, source, cost, and these notes may perhaps be added inoffensively and inconspicuously, though library practice tends increasingly to minimize the amount of such information entered in the book itself. Some owners content themselves with a pencil note on a flyleaf or other blank page, on a margin of a leaf, on a bookplate, others religiously refusing to mark their books in any way and recording the necessary information on the catalog card, shelf list, or similar document. It is a matter for the individual to settle, no council or supreme court having thus far been invested with authority to speak for all.

Many libraries have bookplates and book traditions that add distinction to any volume once on their shelves. Gifts to institutional libraries certainly deserve recognition of the donor by an appropriate plate, both as a form of appreciation and as an encouragement to other possible benefactors. With most books, however, it is safe to say that the less the marking the less the danger of harm.

The private collector is likely sooner or later to wish to have his own bookplate, and it cannot be denied that such plates often add rather than detract from the books they are placed in. It may be pointed out that the more discriminating the collector, the smaller and less ostentatious the plate or label is likely to be.

To be sure, if absence of marking increases the danger of theft, the decision is simple. Some owners use a code in referring to source and price, adopt a cryptic method of marking ownership by notation on certain inside pages, and thus lessen the danger of harm to the volume. The owner undoubtedly has the legal right to add his signature to the flyleaf, or even title page; approval or objection will depend on the point of view of the person making comment.

STAMPS. Perforating stamps or rubber stamps are occasionally used, more often in public collections than private. Little defense can be offered except the obvious hope or belief that the book with them is more likely to be spared a distressing fate than one without. It is difficult to understand how the librarian who has read Randolph G. Adams' classic essay on "Librarians as Enemies of Books"—as every librarian should— can subject books to the indignities of marking and perforation sometimes encountered.

It is possible to have designed and executed rubber stamps of a size and appearance which are not necessarily ugly or forbidding: we should not become discouraged too readily in our quest for them. But this does not justify their use on the title page of the book itself: applied to the verso of the leaf, they will serve their purpose equally as well.

LIFE ON THE SHELVES. When these preliminary records and steps have been finished comes the next hazard in the shape of the life of the book on the shelves. It may be recalled that originally books (or bound manuscripts in codex form) were designed not to stand upright but to lie flat on their sides, the ideal position. Vertical shelving is a space-saving compromise. Because the weight of the paper in a book shelved upright normally pulls away from the spine, it is desirable that books be supported by one another, on shelves reasonably filled, or by means of book supports. If, however, the shelves are too full, it means rubbing and friction when books are forced in or removed. If on the other hand the shelf is not full enough, the books will lean to one side or the other, and the bindings will be harmed.

This seems so slight a matter as frequently to be overlooked, but there is no more insidious or harmful enemy of books than the practice of letting them sag on the shelves. If there are pamphlets or paperbound volumes among the lot their life is certainly neither long nor merry unless they are properly supported.

BOOK SUPPORTS. Book supports can be bought from any dealer in library supplies, or any man handy with tools can make them. You need nothing more than an upright held in position firmly enough to assure an upright position to the books next it. Commercial supports are frequently stamped out of a piece of metal cut in the center and bent to form an upright section. Some have a flange and others not; the former are preferable, since the flange helps to prevent the damage done when books are inadvertently pushed against the support as they are put on the shelf. Those with a hook protruding through the bottom of the shelf must be guarded against to make certain that they do not harm tall books shelved below.

A homemade support can easily be made by taking a piece of seven-eights soft wood four or five inches long and four or five inches wide, with a two by two by four block set at its base. Or a piece of sheet metal may be set against such a base. In many ways the support used in the old Gore Hall days of the Harvard College Library cannot be bettered, and it was nothing but a common clay brick covered with stout paper. These homemade varieties suffer in comparison with commercial supports because of bulkiness and waste of space, but to some booklovers their human touch has a distinct appeal as compared with the more efficient machine product.

HOW BOOKS SHOULD NOT BE SHELVED. One of the quickest and surest ways to damage books is to shelve them on their fore edges, where the weight of the paper pulls by force of gravity from the sewing at the spine. Where this is permitted, a high percentage of rebinding costs can be attributed to it. In the treatment of outsize books, it should be remembered that a book should not be sacrificed to a preconceived classification scheme, whatever the intellectual delights the latter may offer.

Large books should be stored on shelves deep enough to hold them safely, on shelves fitted with proper supports, where the volumes can also support one another and not sag. No exact figures can be set down as marking the precise size that ought to be kept flat on roller (or smooth metal) shelves rather than stand upright, but there is no doubt that large volumes should be stored in a way to minimize friction in shelving or withdrawing them, should be kept upright or flat, never halfway, should be stored in a way to do no damage to themselves or to others.

Similar special treatment should be accorded to miniature books, which if shelved with normal-sized books fail to give the larger volumes needed support and are themselves in danger of being abused and browbeaten by their neighbors.

In the treatment of books of unusual size in institutional

libraries, part of the difficulty is that the standard classification schemes make no provision for books shelved away from their normal location. Some libraries place cards or wooden blocks as "dummies" on the shelves to indicate that such books are shelved elsewhere, but the cards have a way of being over-looked, while the wooden blocks are not always taken seriously. Some libraries incorporate size locations in the call number of their books: at the Houghton Library at Harvard, by pre-fixing the letters "f" (for "folio"), "pf" (for "portfolio") or "m" (for "miniature") before the classification number, a solution which has many merits and permits the cataloguer to participate in the preservation of books. Where the shelf list for the collection also serves as a classified index, a sup-plementary card can be provided under the normal class number.

BOOKS IN EXHIBITION CASES. When books are displayed in exhibition cases care should be taken that the pleasure they provide is not also occasion for serious damage. Above all, direct sunlight should not be allowed to fall on them. The pages exposed to view should be changed now and then, to equalize the harm from exposure. The cases themselves should be dustproof, and if they are, the books are in effect protected by the stable condition of the air. A greater danger arises when the cases are illuminated by electricity, with its accom-panying heat. Because of this, some libraries provide special air conditioning for their exhibition cases; others might place a bowl of water in the cases where this is feasible. The recent experience of the Free Library of Philadelphia where sulphur used in the cork composition lining the cases blackened the silver used in an early illuminated manuscript reveals moreover the care which must be used in drawing up specifications for such cases.

Leather-bound books are particularly liable to damage in the exhibition case. Their normal state is a closed position, and where the leather has been pared at the hinges in binding, the leather is under a strain which can have serious effects over a prolonged period of time. Such harm can be reduced somewhat by oiling the bindings before and after placing them on exhibition, and at intervals if they remain there any length of time.

For holding books open, or pages in place, there are various possible methods. Few libraries can provide the specially designed plastic guards and cords employed by the Pierpont Morgan Library for its travelling exhibition of early books and manuscripts. Small rectangles of plate glass may be used, but their weight should not put undue pressure on the hinges of books which are tightly bound. Such pressure can be relieved by providing supports for the sides in the form of wedge-shaped blocks of wood.

In place of glass, pages may also be held flat by means of soft twine or yarn, tied loosely so that the paper or binding will not be cut: nylon yarn is particularly suitable. Or one may use strips of cellulose acetate foil held down by thumb-tacks. But make sure that it is cellulose acetate and not cellulose nitrate or celluloid. Though the dangers have perhaps been exaggerated, papers which have been in contact with celluloid have been known to disintegrate. The use of elastic bands for holding books open can scarcely be recommended, since the rubber contains sulphur.

Where plates are guarded by tissue paper, the latter may be carefully rolled around a glass rod of appropriate diameter: the weight of the rod will keep the paper in place in the inner margin. In this a certain skill may be required, but it is possible.

In this context one might also mention the danger the librarian encounters in showing his treasures to visitors. How easy it is to take from the shelves again and again the same striking and spectacular volumes! Imagination and self-discipline are of help in resisting the frequent handling of the identical volumes, and should be developed—a happier solution than pretending that the keys of the bookcases have been temporarily mislaid.

CARE IN HANDLING BOOKS. The private library suffers less danger to books while being handled than does the public collection with volumes bandied about between ignorant readers and thoughtless attendants. How few people avoid pulling a book from the shelves by the top of its spine, weakening the cloth or leather; how few people can resist the temptation to lay an open book upside down, instead of using a bookmark; how many people are indifferent to their choice of bookmarks themselves; how many people see no harm in writing upon the surface of a page, despite the indentations it leaves!

In the private home, housecleaning or moving does more harm to books than their normal use under ordinary circumstances. In the larger institutional collections they suffer sadly unless subject to constant, intelligent, sympathetic supervision. Few things are more dangerous than stacking books into shaky, unstable piles; a slight jar and they tumble to the floor. Tossing books like tennis balls may conceivably amuse youngsters, but it gives little benefit to the victims.

In general, a respect for books as physical objects can perhaps best be inculcated by example: the librarian who is indifferent to their care can scarcely expect his subordinates to surpass him in care. It may be added, moreover, that there appears to be a curious correlation between the care which books are accorded in a library and the over-all morale of the institution: the condition of the bookstacks becomes a valid measure of the self-respect and devotion of the library staff as a whole.

PACKING. If books have to be moved the idea is to wrap each volume in good kraft wrapping paper, pack them stoutly to prevent friction or rubbing, handle them and their boxes with thoughtful and intelligent care, treat them with the respect they deserve.

If they are packed back to back, fore edge to fore edge, there is danger of flattening rounded backs. If back must be packed against back, lessen the risk by laying sheets of paper or cardboard or other safe packing material in a way to even up the projection of the back. Fore edge of one against edge of the back of the next volume lessens the need of this insertion, but there will still remain the danger of a shift and consequent pressure of rounded back against the plane surface of the other cover. The solution there is to prevent slipping by proper packing and fastening.

Chapter Three

SOME ENEMIES OF BOOKS

THE SAFEGUARDING of books from their enemies is not a form of magic—despite the curses sometimes found entered to that end by their scribes in early manuscripts—but the implementation of accumulated knowledge. Insofar as we acquaint ourselves with the basic principles involved our efforts at preservation will be rewarded and rewarding.

Fortunately, to do so we need not become experts in chemistry, bacteriology, or entomology, though we skirt these fields. But an elementary understanding of the physical properties of the materials of bookmaking will go far to explain the nature of the battle and of the enemies in question.

PAPER. With paper we are dealing, essentially, with an organic substance, cellulose. The cellulose molecule is an extremely complex one, probably made up of a lengthy chain of links, links which by the chemical action of ultraviolet rays or of acids may break into shorter and weaker chains, still cellulose but cellulose of an inferior sort. It may be noted that natural cellulose has a tensile strength which compares favorably with that of aluminum or of silver wire, and it is not surprising that it makes so durable a material.

Although modern technology may yet produce an inexpensive cellulose paper without recourse to nature, paper as we know it today is derived by intermediary stages, from cotton, flax, grasses, straw, or wood.

Whatever its source, the cellulose is subjected to manufacturing processes which may, and often do, introduce other factors which may either preserve or lead to the destruction of the paper. The water employed may or may not be pure; the sizing—either of gelatin or of starch, or involving resin and alum—necessary for a smooth writing surface offers its own hazards. The machinery used may introduce iron into the paper, which catalyzes sulphur dioxide in the air to form sulphuric acid. Not only may chemical reactions result from these elements, but gelatin and starch are also foodstuffs attractive to insect and bacterial growths.

While for many years it was believed that paper made from rags was the most lasting and desirable, it is now acknowledged that the issue is more complicated. Even though rags may have been used, bleaches have at times left acidic residues. Of all the factors most likely to shorten the life of paper, acidity is now considered the greatest. In tests conducted by the National Bureau of Standards and by William Barrow of the Virginia State Library, it has been found that the proportion of acid, measured inversely in terms of pH,* present in paper is the best key to its ability to withstand the passage of time.

It is particularly disconcerting to discover that the papers used in book manufacture in this century have been and continue to be, for the most part, highly acidic (with a pH count of less than 5), and that their disintegration within a matter of decades is a real possibility. Such high acidity of book papers is due largely to the nature of the sizing employed,

* The term "pH" is defined as "a means of expressing the degree of acidity or basicity of a solution. Thus at normal temperature a neutral solution such as pure distilled water has a pH of about 7, a tenth-normal solution of hydrochloric acid . . . has a pH near 1, and a normal solution of a strong alkali such as sodium hydroxide has a pH of nearly 14"—*The Condensed Chemical Dictionary.* 5th ed., rev. by Arthur and Elizabeth Rose (New York, Reinhold, 1956), 845.

but it may be counteracted by submitting them to de-acidification. Whether or not the paper industry will be willing to adopt the steps suggested by Barrow remains to be seen, and in the meantime the preservationist is left to solve his immediate problems as best he can.

INK. The writing substances which have been used in the past divide themselves, generally speaking, into two classes: carbon inks and oak gall inks.

The first of these employs black soot, or lampblack, derived from resinous substances. The tiny black particles are joined with a fluid, such as water, and a binding agent, usually gum arabic. In this there is no chemical action, nor is there likely to be one with paper. The inks used in printing are, for the most part, carbon inks, comprising lampblack mixed with boiled linseed oil to form a suitable paste.

Oak gall inks on the other hand are a compound of oak galls (or other vegetable substance) with ferrous sulphate. The resulting ink produces a chemical and acidic action in proportion to the amount of ferrous sulphate, and may damage paper.

LEATHER. Whether made from the skins of cattle, pigs, sheep, or goats, leather has proven an ideal binding material. The protein molecules constituting leather probably resemble those of cellulose, comprising long chains with shorter side links as well, providing three-dimensional strength. The tanning process used for making a skin pliable greatly affects its durability. In the nineteenth century sulphuric acid was often used in the coloring process, with harmful effects.

CLOTH. The modern book cloth is more often used, of course, than leather for binding, being less expensive and certainly more lasting than poorly tanned leather. Before being used for binding, the cloth is usually sized, with either starch or thin gelatin. Unfortunately the colors used are sometimes not fast; too often they will run or rub off, while in the tropics or humid climates the sizing itself encourages the growth of molds and mildew and attracts insects in their hunger.

In providing book cloths, the binding industry is active in its search for more suitable and attractive materials, and interested particularly in the possible usefulness of newer synthetics, of which we speak in Chapter 8. If librarians sometimes feel that their particular needs are not being met, it may be recalled that commercial bookbinders are not unresponsive but are committed to producing books economically.

PASTES AND GLUE. Used as binding agents in the manufacture of books, paste and glue also play their doubtful part in the survival of paper and leather.

The glue used in the backing of the book is traditionally a gelatinous substance of animal origin. Paste is normally made from flour, either from wheat or rice. But here again technology has made available new adhesives of a synthetic nature, especially polyvinyl acetate, which offer great possibilities.

With the organic character of the book materials in mind we can more readily consider the enemies to which books are prey. Some of these can be seen, and methods of control or remedy may be obvious. But some of the most insidious, persistent, voracious, and insistent attackers cannot be seen in operation, though their effect and results may be plain even to the blind.

HARM FROM SUNLIGHT AND DARKNESS. Sunshine properly employed helps to free our books from various enemies; but sunshine, owing to its heat and to its ultraviolet rays, is also a danger and should not be allowed to fall directly upon bindings or on paper.

It is the ultraviolet rays which are particularly menacing, bombarding as they do the molecular structure of paper and leather. Sometimes the resulting deterioration may be visible, through the fading of the dyes or the browning of the paper, but paper may be so affected without its showing. Where direct sunlight cannot otherwise be avoided, it should be filtered through thick green or yellow glass, which screens out the harmful rays.

Darkness, on the other hand, protects books from the harm of direct light, but when associated with humidity encourages the growth of molds and of insects. In tropical climates the storage of books in dark, hot, and humid quarters will almost inevitably result in attacks upon them by molds or insects: one can expect little else.

HARM FROM THE AIR. The air we breathe may be one of the worst enemies of the books we collect. It harms if too dry, it harms if too wet. When books are kept in rooms with air too dry their paper and leather turn brittle and begin to crumble. This should not happen, to be sure, and would not happen if paper and leather had proper resistance. Paper books and leather bindings have for ages existed in dry climates with no serious harm. But paper and leather in these later days are made to sell rather than to last; cheapness is more essential than permanence. Paper and leather and cloth for books play so small a part in the whole field of the paper and leather and textile industries that librarians are in no position to insist on obedience to their demands, even if these demands were sharply enough defined to be formulated. Good paper and good cloth and good leather can be had, nonetheless, by anyone willing to pay the price properly demanded. If equally good craftsmen to employ them are difficult to find, it is perhaps because too few people have been able or willing to pay their appropriate hire.

HARM FROM DAMPNESS. Excessive humidity, which prevails in so many parts of the world, is but one of the concrete factors in deterioration. Too much dampness means mold and mildew, the loosening of paste and glue, the weakening of paper and leather, and is a real problem not only in the tropics but in regions where fog and mist are normal.

The remedy is essentially that of removing the humidity—howsoever difficult this may sometimes seem. It may be done by artificial heat, by the increased circulation of dry air, or by the use of electrically operated dehumidifiers. Within small enclosed areas, such as a cupboard or closet, anhydrous calcium chloride may be used to absorb moisture, placed in bowls or in hanging wire containers especially made for the purpose. From time to time the moisture it has absorbed must be expelled by baking it.

HARM FROM DRYNESS. Many libraries in the United States will have more trouble in fostering and cultivating humidity than in driving it away. The prevalence of central heating may make winter tolerable for human beings but it is harmful for books. European booksellers have been known to view regretfully the sale of finely bound books to American clients, as they envisage the fate of the bindings in our hot dry homes. For dry heat drives the life out of the paper and leather, and calls for mitigation of its dryness by artificial moistening of the air.

This is largely a matter of attention, thoughtfulness, and care in the ordinary household, or of the artificial conditioning of air in larger structures and institutions; it is another instance of the real need for air conditioning in the library. If a house is heated by a hot-air furnace it is usually simple to add hot water to the air as it leaves the firebox. With steam and hot-water heating, other methods must be used. Various devices are on the market for attachment to radiators, to be filled with water and thus increase the humidity by evaporation. Some are simple, requiring little more than a daily thought to keep them filled; others are more complicated. The counterpart of the dehumidifier may also be employed, the electrically operated humidifier.

Some librarians have found satisfactory results from setting wet sponges in copper receptacles under their bookcases. Others have turned to open vessels treated as furniture or pieces of ornament. As a matter of fact, the means is perhaps less important than the end, the securing of an average humidity of 50 or 60 per cent.

The electric humidifiers and dehumidifiers currently marketed normally incorporate humidistatic control. Otherwise a hygrometer, to measure the humidity, and a wet-and-dry-bulb thermometer, which cost little and are simple to read, are essential: else the measures employed may degenerate into meaningless window dressing. Occasional use of a hygrometer, followed up by efforts to take advantage of what it tells, will benefit any collection of books. Bear in mind, however, that a great deal of water has to evaporate to affect the humidity of a room heated to 70 degrees in cold weather. Keeping the temperature down is an excellent way to keep the relative humidity up.

HARM FROM DUST. There are all sorts of dust, from the lint given off by clothing to the small particles of soot or of sand carried by the passing wind. Tiny though they may be, they are not too small to cut fine leather; they may, moreover, serve as a nucleus for acidic vapor. Against such dust, however, electrostatic filters may provide some relief.

POLLUTED AIR. It is more difficult to ward off the attacks of noxious gases, more difficult to learn of their presence before their effects show themselves, more difficult to remove them or to keep them out, quite as difficult to repair their ravages. Yet studies of the deterioration of books show it to be in direct relation to their vicinity to industrially polluted air. For gases either in themselves or in combination with book materials can produce chemical reactions and the breakdown of paper and bindings. This is especially true of sulphur dioxide, which, in the presence of iron in paper or leather, becomes sulphuric acid, with all its corrosive effects. Against such fumes electrostatic filters are inadequate, and washing the air is essential.

Here again we have an argument in behalf of air conditioning, which is no longer a counsel of perfection for
the institutional library. For the small householder the only
refuge may be to change his residence. If he lives near a
laundry or smelter or power plant, or any one of a dozen other
lethal instruments developed by our civilization, he may be
sure that day by day and hour by hour their chimneys and
smokestacks belch forth gases that pollute the air and are
certain to take their toll of anything in his house composed
wholly or partly of leather or paper. The city dweller is of
course in a much worse situation in this respect than his
brother in the country far removed from evidence of modern
industrial progress. Community control of sewage disposal has
progressed farther than community control of atmosphere
pollution, though steps are perforce being taken in this
direction as well.

An owner of good books who becomes aware that he is
living in a region subject to this air pollution will do well
to think about his responsibility toward his books as well as his
family. The institutional library, when seemingly free of air
pollution in a suburban location, or elsewhere, should bear
in mind possible shifts in industrial growth, and in planning
new buildings at least make provision by vents and duct space
against the possible future need for air conditioning.

AIR-BORNE DISEASE GERMS. Disease-laden air is not
infrequently charged with blame for damage to books. Just
how much harm can be done to books by air-borne disease
germs is doubtful. An eye is frequently cast askance on books
used by the sick or on books housed in rooms where sickness
has laid its hand. It is perhaps not unnatural to assume that
modern precautions would recommend disinfection, but it
is safe to say that few cases of infection can be traced un-
questionably to books. Studies conducted in Italy give assurance
to this view.

The best judgment calls for burning of books contaminated
by anthrax and smallpox; for other contagious diseases ex-

posure to fresh air and to sunlight (however deleterious to the books themselves) may remove any remaining misgivings.

TUBERCULOSIS. Every now and then some earnest soul feels oppressed by the danger to the community from books belonging to public libraries used by persons suffering from tuberculosis. The consensus now held by competent medical men seems to be that tuberculosis cannot be spread in this way.

VERMIN, INSECTS, AND MOLDS. While sunlight, heat, humidity, and gases are harmful to books, there exist other agents to be guarded against, particularly in the form of animal and vegetable life. And where there is no air conditioning there is indeed real danger. Books are attractive to insects and vermin as well as to molds and mildew because of the food value they offer, less in the cellulose of paper itself than in the paste, glue, gelatin, and similar products used in the finishing of the paper and the binding.

To forestall such attacks is a far happier course than to destroy the attacker after he has appeared; and the maintenance of heat and humidity within optimum limits is the best deterrent. Chemicals which by their odor deter the approach of insects are to be preferred to those which kill only after damage has been done. In the case of modern insecticides, even when they do not damage or discolor the material to be protected, it must be borne in mind that insects have been known to build up immunity to them through succeeding generations. At the same time one cannot wholly discard some of the folk remedies found in some parts of the world. In India, for instance, it is believed that wrapping material in red or yellow cloth will keep insects away. Too little is known on the matter to say that this is not the case, but it is no doubt owing to some chemical property of the dye and not to the color. The wiser course is to make use of chemicals as such.

Against vermin such as mice and rats the usual household remedies should in normal situations be adequate. If the need

arises, a professional exterminator may be called in, but he should be competent, and aware of the problems involved in treating book materials.

In general, spraying, not of the books but of walls and shelves against insects with DDT, Dieldrin, or similar insecticides may be employed if one recognizes that they are volatile substances and that the process will have to be repeated from time to time (more often in the tropics than in temperate zones). Bracey and Barlow, in England, have devised a lacquer containing insecticides which, applied to bookshelves, has been effective in killing book pests. Although it may be used as a lacquer on books, it discolors leather, and users are strongly warned against applying it to valuable or old bindings. (*Journal of Documentation, 9*, 157-68.)

There are various insects which have an affinity for books, and the literature relating to them is extensive. The most comprehensive account (with bibliography) is that prepared by Harry Weiss and R. H. Carruthers. Of those insects most generally encountered it is possible to speak briefly.

SILVER FISH. Temperate climates do not encourage the growth of insect life in libraries, but even here one will occasionally find a small insect, the silver fish (taking its name from its color), which is attracted by glue and paste as well as by the gelatin with which photographs and highly coated papers are sized.

Of the various means of destroying silver fish, apart from maintaining a high degree of cleanliness, the simplest remedy is perhaps to spread a mixture of boric acid and flour where they are likely to encounter it. If a more drastic approach is called for, then a mixture of 12 parts of sodium fluoride in 100 parts of flour may be used, bearing in mind that sodium fluoride is poisonous to human beings as well. If the spreading of powder is inconvenient or unsightly, a simple expedient practiced at the University of California at Los Angeles may instead be used; this consists of jelly glasses placed at yard intervals, with masking tape or similar adhesive in strips up

the outside of each. Inside a teaspoon of flour is placed. The silver fish are able to climb into the glass to get at the flour, but trapped inside, cannot crawl out again.

COCKROACHES. Equally widespread is the cockroach, which while preferring sweet foods will in desperation attack books. Commercial insecticides, or the sodium fluoride mixture suggested for silver fish, may be used against it.

BOOKWORMS. Although the bookworm is rarely found in temperate climates, it is not to be written off altogether, since it occasionally makes its appearance as far north as Boston. Its true home is in tropical and semitropical climates.

The damage done by bookworms occurs in the larva stage of the life cycle of a large variety of beetles, numbering over thirty, which lay their eggs on the spines or edges of books. On hatching, the larvae eat their way into the book, feeding particularly upon the paste and the glue they find there. Presently the larvae develop through the pupal stage to become beetles and to repeat the cycle.

Against the larvae and the beetles poison and fumigation are effective. Naphthalene in the form of blocks or paradichlorobenzene crystals will give off fumes which will repel the beetles. Books in which live bookworms have been found may be put into an airproof cabinet or container with paradichlorobenzene crystals. At a temperature of 70 degrees the crystals, in a proportion of one pound for each 10 cubic feet, will give off fumes which will kill most insects, provided the books or other materials are arranged to permit the ready circulation of the fumes. The material should remain in the container for at least a fortnight.

Unfortunately paradichlorobenzene does not kill the eggs, and on removal material thus fumigated should be segregated for at least another three weeks and watched for the appearance of larvae before it is returned to its regular shelves. Against eggs only vacuum fumigation has been found successful, a measure feasible only in the largest of libraries where there is constant need for it, such as the Huntington Library in California.

TERMITES. Against termites (or white ants) the best prevention is architectural: the provision of a building which is free of wooden surfaces in contact with the soil. Some termites cannot live without a life line connected with damp earth, and in darkness, although they may build for themselves enclosed passageways above ground for short distances; others, unfortunately, can live in dryness. The habits of termites, which are able to feed on wood and paper due to the presence in their digestional tracts of enzyme-producing parasites, are sufficiently well known to permit effective safeguards against them. But even so they are increasingly a menace; while closed during World War II the Vatican Library suffered from their inroads.

MILDEW OR MOLD. Mildew or mold is a direct result of dampness and high temperature. It appears as a thin, whitish coating of fungi of various kinds, and its action is unbelievably swift as it feeds upon the gelatinous sizing of books and paper. The best remedy is prevention, and the best prevention is storage in light, well-ventilated rooms where books are kept dry. All easy enough to say, to be sure, but what help has any owner of books against the humid heat that occasionally swoops down on helpless residents of some areas, or during the seasonal monsoons? Well, for one thing, he can shut windows and turn on artificial heat or his dehumidifier, no matter what the thermometer says as to the outside temperature. He must first drive away the humidity. Heat may be uncomfortable, but if it is dry the mold will not spread. Then rub the books with clean, dry cloths and keep careful watch to see that no advance takes place.

Another means of prevention which has found favor in tropical climates is to coat the books with lacquer (see Chapter 7), which prevents the growth of molds on the gelatinous sizing of cloths. While for books destined for tropical libraries special materials would be desirable, this is another case where the demand has not yet justified action. It has been noted, however, that book cloths of green and yellow color seem less conducive to mildew growths than those which are black, dark blue, or red.

Many cases of mold or mildew can be removed from paper by alcohol if the stain is on the surface, but the danger of alcohol's doing damage must in turn be borne in mind.

THYMOL FUMIGATION. In recent years fumigation with thymol has proven a satisfactory measure, both as a preventive and as a remedy for molds and mildew. Here again an airtight chamber is necessary, fitted with racks of stainless steel and an electric light of 100-watts intensity. Over the light a shallow glass dish is placed containing thymol crystals. The heat from the light is sufficient to vaporize the crystals, the thymol fumes destroying the mold. How long the material should be kept in the container—from a day or two to a week —will depend on the severity of the attack. Needless to say, the thymol crystals should be kept in supply in the glass dish. Since thymol evaporates readily and its effects do not last, treatment may need to be repeated from time to time.

DUSTING AND CLEANING. Man too is a potential biological enemy of books, and one of his most malevolent and hostile acts against them may be well-intentioned dusting or cleaning. Books ought to be kept clean, of course. No lover of books wants them to soil fingers or clothes or anything else connected with the reader. But no lover of books can ever think with any other emotion than horror and dread when he considers their fate during spring or fall housecleaning. Dust on books may be unsightly, but it certainly can do no such harm as the banging and thumping they receive on these occasions. A vacuum cleaner will remove dust, granted it is properly designed and is fitted with a proper brush with long soft bristles, and is handled with a modicum of intelligence and respect. The sort of nozzle is perhaps less important than that care be taken that the bristle not scratch leather or cloth, or that metal not scrape the binding. Dust cloths will remove dust if lightly used: they should not be employed to grind the dust into the books themselves. Here as in various other processes, the instrument is less important than the judgment that governs its use.

If it should prove to be a choice between permitting dust to accumulate and seeing the shelves and books cleaned in ordinary slapdash fashion, there is little doubt as to the wisdom of choosing the former as one considers the damage to bindings, the dust ground inexorably into covers and papers, or merely redistributed to settle elsewhere. How successful the owner proves to be in carrying out his choice is largely a matter of personality. Uncontrolled cleaning zeal can do much harm to books.

REGULAR SUPERVISION. Just as guardians of public health are more anxious to ensure proper precautions and to develop preventive medicine than to indulge in heroic measures of restoration after disease has set in, so the owner of a library will fare much better if he has the books examined now and then by a competent craftsman to repair slight defects before they develop, and to help these mute companions of his quiet hours, these helpers in his efforts to spread knowledge of human life and thought, resist the baneful influences that snap at them from every corner of the room and from every pair of hands that stretches toward them. It is a comparatively easy matter to see that leather bindings are kept in good condition; or, at least, it is much more easy to start afresh and see that they do not go backward, than it is to repair the damage when once it has begun its wicked work. Find a competent person—with an instinctive affection for books as physical objects—and set him at a systematic examination of shelf after shelf, let him patch here and repair there as the patients call for help and attention, and at the end of the year the books will be in much better condition than if the need of the binder's care is called to mind only when the case is so striking as to shriek its demands.

Chapter Four

THE REPAIR AND
MENDING OF BOOKS

SKILL IN MENDING books depends to a certain extent on the knowledge the mender has of the way in which books are made. The more one knows about bookbinding materials, leather, paper, cloth, thread, paste, and glue, the better the chances of success. How will the paper wear? Is it brittle or tough? How do paste and glue affect it? Knowledge of these and similar points joined to practice in mending and repairing, will help mightily.

One is sometimes tempted to extend Punch's advice about marriage to the problem of mending books. Many books, to be sure, repaired by inexperienced hands, or with improper materials, have been so sadly harmed that their old age is much worse than their youth. Far better to set them aside and wrap them up till they can be turned over to competent and understanding hands. Sometimes, even, it is better, for the purpose they serve, not to replace their original materials, comprising evidence of value to scholars. But in many cases the life of books can be materially lengthened if intelligent first aid is given as soon as signs of ill-health appear. After a book begins to break, its lesions call for practiced care and attention quite as obviously as torn skin or broken bones on the human frame.

Book anatomy is not so complex or intricate as that of the upper vertebrates, to be sure, but the surgeon must have sympathy and training whether treating books or man.

ANATOMY OF THE BOOK. There is no reason, however, why the average collector and lover of books should not make minor repairs—after he has learned how books are put together. His introduction to book anatomy should begin with the dissection of useless cadavers rather than with attempts at vivisection. Take an old book obviously on its way to the waste basket, and see how much you can learn by study of its construction before you begin to use the knife. Note how the board or leather covers or backs have a layer of cloth or paper pasted down them for protection and ornament. See how the back is sometimes the same sheet as the cover, sometimes is another sheet of leather or cloth. Learn how the covers are fastened to the book. In modern books you will see this connection is merely a thin sheet of "super" or muslin glued to the signatures on its one side and to the boards on the other. Come to know the difference between the sewing of signatures or gatherings on cords and the overcasting of signatures to one another by stitches that may or may not hold securely. See whether the plates are pasted on or are folded in. Careful study and observation will help to avoid many mistakes in attempting repairs, while familiarity with the theory of binding, as set forth by Douglas Cockerell in his *Bookbinding, and the Care of Books,* will explain many other details.

QUALITY OF MATERIALS. In undertaking repairs of books not only are intelligence and manual skills required, but it is essential as well that the materials used be of a quality commensurate to their use. How disheartening it is to see extraordinary craftsmanship expended upon materials which are unstable, containing within themselves the seeds of their own destruction and potentially harmful as well to the books they seek to protect.

It is especially necessary that the leather and paper employed be of acceptable standard. Thus, in selecting one's leather, it is important that the defects of badly tanned skins be avoided. One way in which this may be achieved is to secure those which have been prepared in England and meet the N.I.R.A. test of the British Leather Manufacturers' Association. Or information about acid-resistant leathers may be obtained from the United States Department of Agriculture, Eastern Utilization Branch, Philadelphia 18, Pennsylvania.

For paper it was formerly thought sufficient to specify an "all rag" stock, but today such a view is at best an over-simplification of the matter. It is more important that paper be free of too high a proportion of acid. That is, it should have a pH value of not less than 5, while its alpha cellulose content should be at least 90 per cent. Unfortunately we are at the mercy of our suppliers: it is easier to demand than to secure these standards. Where the amount of paper to be purchased justifies the step, samples may be submitted to chemical testing firms which undertake this work, such as the Skinner and Sherman Company of Newton, Massachusetts. University libraries may perhaps turn to their chemistry departments for this service. And we can all hope that the day will come when library supply houses will be prepared to guarantee the stability of the materials they offer for sale in such terms, rather than in the general phrase of "rag" content.

ADHESIVES. When repair work really begins one of the first things needed is an adhesive—glue, paste, or one of the new synthetics. Books may be made without paper; many are made of leather or vellum and little else. Books may be made without cloth or parchment or binder's boards. But it is difficult, not to say impossible, to make them without some form of binding agent.

GLUE. Glue is an organic substance obtained from skins, hides, bones, sinews of neat cattle, sheep, horses, and other animals; some comes from the heads and bones of fish. Hide glue is usually supposed to give the best adhesive qualities. Glue differs from paste in that it can be made to remain flexible, at normal temperatures, when dry. Paste always dries brittle. It is the addition of glycerine and other elements that permits glue to dry flexible. Because it contains less moisture in its usable state and because it dries more quickly after application, glue has advantages over paste in various kinds of work. For the backs of books flexible glue is usually employed, because it will dry and remain strong, elastic, capable of bending without cracking. Under such conditions paste would be brittle when dry. So too the joints will soon crack, sometimes break, when they are opened or shut if a hard, brittle glue has been used. A high-grade glue will have less odor, will be stronger, will cover more space than one of poorer quality.

Glue is usually bought in flakes, sheets, cakes, or pulverized form. It is heated in a gas or electric pot, and it should be softened by soaking it in water before applying heat. As it burns easily, a double boiler type of pot is usually best for heating; the danger of burning is thus avoided, and the hot water serves to retain the heat even after the original heater is turned off. The commercial bindery uses glue pots or glueing machines, which permit heat to be supplied constantly with accurate measurement or adjustment.

POLYVINYL ACETATE ADHESIVES. Of the synthetic adhesives developed in recent years one of the most promising has been polyvinyl acetate, which has made possible the phenomenal spread of the paperback book with its "perfect" binding. Polyvinyl acetate is of interest not only to the mass manufacturer of books but also to the restorer of books as well. It can be used in the repair of books wherever glue is likely to be called for, and has the added merit that, not being a foodstuff, it is not attractive to insects.

Although as acetate is used in the production of books heat may be required for applying it in sheets to bindings, it is also available in emulsion form, which does not require heat. A whitish liquid, it is available commercially packaged under various names, as "Liquick Leather," "Elmer's Glue-All," "Bind-Art," and the like; the large consumer may find it more economical to by-pass such packaging and purchase his supplies direct from the numerous producers of the emulsion as such.

In its emulsion form polyvinyl acetate may be applied with a brush, care being taken that when not in actual use the brush be kept in water lest it harden (when this does occur a solvent such as acetone can be employed). The commercial liquid may come in a consistency not suitable for its particular use, generally being somewhat thick, but it may be thinned by the addition of water. Unlike glue, however, which can be removed by the application of hot water or steam, the removal of polyvinyl acetate is more difficult, once it has set. Admittedly there remains a resistance to the use of polyvinyl acetate on the part of some bookmen, and its claims have perhaps been exaggerated in a first fling of enthusiasm. But used judiciously, it has nonetheless won acceptance as a valuable means of repair.

PASTE. Paste is made from flour obtained from the grains of rye, wheat, corn, or rice; from the husks, cobs, stalks of some of these plants; from various starches, dextrins, and sometimes from gums. It is one of the first essentials in any bindery. It differs from glue in having a greater moisture content, in drying more slowly by evaporation. Paste is usually white, or nearly so, and it does not stain as glue is likely to do. It shares with glue the disadvantage that it is a foodstuff, and attractive to insects.

WHEN TO USE PASTE OR GLUE. The experienced binder is rarely in doubt as to when to use paste or glue, though he may wonder about polyvinyl acetate. Paste is chosen for paper and soft cloths, such as cambric, canton flannel, silk; for casing-in books, for end leaves, for mending and repairing torn pages. Glue (or polyvinyl acetate) is used for the backs of books, and for colored or sized book-covering cloths. If paste should be applied to some book cloths its moisture would soften the cloth and remove color, size, grain. Binder's boards and leather permit either glue or paste, with due consideration to the kind of work and the results desired. On books bound in quarter or half leather flexible glue is normally used. Books bound in three-quarter leather or full leather, with raised bands, call for paste, because it is slow in drying and permits the binder more time to handle the whole process. With books of this kind glue would prevent satisfactory handling of the leather, because it dries so quickly that the binder would not have time enough to stretch and pull and form the leather.

MAKING PASTE. Paste may be made out of flour and water, the success of the effort depending largely on the skill and experience of the hands that do the mixing. In general it will be simplest to buy the paste on sale by any reliable stationer or dealer in library or binding supplies. The only difference between the paste you make and the paste you buy is that the commercial paste has a bit of preservative added to prevent its becoming rancid—but this you may do yourself as well.

For the satisfaction some of us get out of actually seeing things grow and take shape, paste may be mixed in any convenient bowl. Begin on a small scale and take about half a cup of flour. Add cold water gradually, stirring constantly until water and flour are blended, all the lumps smoothed out, and the mixture just about the proper consistency for gravy, for instance, not so fluid as soup, not as viscous as bread dough. Then add boiling water, put on the fire, and bring the mass to a boil for about one minute, stirring constantly. If it becomes too thick, add sufficient hot water to bring it to proper consistency. Count on its thickening 10 to 15 per cent as it cools. It should not run so freely as milk, should not be lumpy, should not be so stiff as to fail to run from the brush with moderate ease. Starch may be used instead of flour; it is entirely a matter of preference, price, and convenience. If a preservative is desired, thymol crystals (in a minute amount) may be added.

Where insects and molds are a problem, the formula for paste developed by the National Archives of India may be

employed, as a means of overcoming the attraction paste offers
to insect life:

Dextrine flour	5	lbs.
Water	10	lbs.
Oil of cloves	1.5	ozs.
Saffrol	1.5	ozs.
Lead carbonate	2.5	ozs.

The resulting paste is poisonous to human beings as well as
to insects, and workers using it should be fully aware of its
dangers if taken internally.

Dry paste can also be bought in pound packages or larger
quantities, requiring little more attention than adding water
and stirring. This is what most paper hangers use. The commercial binder frequently mixes his paste in a machine, using
special flour that permits adding hot water at once; but he
uses paste in quantities far beyond the needs of the reader who
turns to this book for help.

However, even if commercial paste is more satisfactory,
do not adopt it exclusively until you have made enough paste
to satisfy yourself that you can actually make it. You certainly should learn by experience how much moisture is
best for your work; the drier the paste the less danger of
wrinkling, but if too dry it will not bind.

In using paste remember that the less you use the better.
The normal tendency is to use too much. A thin coat of any
adhesive firmly pressed into the pores of the objects to be
joined will hold the sheets more successfully than a thicker
lot that has little more than its own portions to stick to and
rapidly grows weaker and more brittle the drier it gets.

Remember too that paste contains moisture, which means
that the pasted sheet has a tendency to curl or wrinkle, especially in dry rooms. Pressure is needed to force the paste into
the paper fiber, for one thing, and for another to keep the
paper smooth while it dries. If too much paste is applied it
will squeeze out beyond the edges, which may cause other

pages to stick together or may soil portions difficult to clean. Experience and experiment will show when there is too little or too much, when it is too thin or stiff. The more practice on books and paper that mean little, the more certain is good work on books and paper that mean much.

Paste may be applied with thumb or finger if nothing better is near, but in the long run a good brush pays for itself. Paste brushes are made of the hair of horsetails, pigs, wild boars, the last the best. They are softer than glue brushes, flat rather than round like glue brushes, need little care and attention other than regular cleaning after use, and ought to last for a long time. Hang them up when not in use, or keep them flat, to avoid forcing the hairs to take a "set" and get permanently out of shape.

REPAIR EQUIPMENT. And that brings up the question of the working area and of materials and equipment in general. The best work cannot be accomplished in ill-lit, cramped, and disorganized quarters, either overheated or drafty. Means of heating materials, a good-sized sink, and supplies of water should be close at hand. Shelves and cupboards should permit the neat and dustproof storage of materials. The craftsman, who knows his needs best, should, within reason, be encouraged to make his needs known, rather than be forced in desperation to beg.

The primary essential is a table, kitchen or otherwise, offering a level, smooth working space at a convenient height, 30 to 36 inches from the floor, depending on whether you prefer to work sitting or standing. The materials noted below may be secured from any supply house dealing in bookbinding materials. Some dealers in library supplies sell repair kits and mending outfits put up in handy and attractive containers:

Bone folders, 2 or 3
Knives, one with the usual cutting edge, one with bevel edge
    for paring
Scissors, one with 5-inch blades, one with 7-inch blades

Sheet zinc, for cutting cloth, leather, and paper
Straight edge, about 18 inches long
Plate glass sheets, about 18 inches square
Paste brushes and paste pot
Sponges, several
Book papers, of several kinds
Blotting and wax paper
Bond paper, for guarding plates
Tissue paper (Japanese) for mending
Cambric and book cloth, several yards
Scales
Book press, about 12 by 15 inches in size
Photographer's developing trays
Finishing press, to hold normally sized volumes
Weights, which can be easily made by covering bricks with
    kraft paper.

TORN PAGES. Torn pages probably mark the first injury
to a book, and they may be mended in any of the following
ways.

If the tear does not affect the printing, cut a strip of thin but
tough paper half an inch wide, a little longer than the tear.
Cover the strip with paste and then lay it carefully on the
paper over the tear, being sure to see that both edges of the
tear have been brought together evenly. The strip should
project slightly beyond the tear on the sound side of the paper
and slightly beyond the edge also; trim the overhang along the
edge with a pair of shears or scissors. A good way to paste
mending strips is to spread the paste evenly on a piece of glass
and lay the strip on it. Lift the strip and enough paste should
adhere to it, just enough, not too much or too little.

When the tear extends into the print, put a small bit of
paste on the torn edges and place them together. Then take a
piece of soft mending tissue and rub it gently over the tear
in a way to make the tissue adhere to the torn edges. Then
put the paper into the book press or under a weight until it
is dry. Tear off the superfluous tissue, taking care always to

pull toward the tear from both sides. The delicate, soft fibers of the tissue act as a binder, and when the task has been well done it is almost impossible to see how the mend has been accomplished. Here again it is practice that counts, and the first efforts should be made with books and torn pages that can afford to be spoiled.

REPAIR OF NEWSPAPERS. The private library will but rarely have newspapers to be treated, and under ordinary circumstances such volumes should go to the professional binder, if repair is justified at all. While the bibliophile shudders at the destruction of the book or printed materials in any form, the newspaper, once it began its career on wood pulp paper, became for preservation purposes practically a lost cause. Its inevitable disintegration calls for putting the text on microfilm as quickly as possible.

COVERING MATERIALS. Printed or manuscript sheets will often be given longer life if they are covered with some protecting fabric. This means lessening of legibility, in many cases, to be sure, but the protection of the surface is usually well worth the price. For the unusually valuable or important document the extra precaution of having a photostat made of it before submitting it to treatment will frequently be justified. And legibility need not be reduced to an improper extent if judgment, care, and good materials are used. When the alternative is the disintegration into uselessness of the piece itself, one has little choice.

Though such treatment may, in cases of emergency, be given to sheets in a bound volume, the ideal is to take the book apart and handle the sheets flat. Silk or Japanese tissue paper have traditionally been the favored materials. "Silking"—the covering of paper with silk or chiffon—costs more and does less harm to legibility than the paper, although the material may yellow or become brittle with the passage of time, and can only with difficulty be removed for replacement. Tissue costs less, is not so transparent as silk, but gives more protection from the air. When either is used, both sides of the paper are usually covered in American practice, to prevent curling, owing to the unbalanced pull of the covered side when but one is treated. Elsewhere, where there is greater normal humidity, a single side alone may be covered.

PASTE. For an adhesive, make a flour paste with a small quantity of tapioca dextrin added, the thinner the better. But if it is too thin it will not bind, and if it is too thick it shows lumps and gives an uneven result. Experience and good judgment are the only guides. Some paper, moreover, calls for thin paste and some for thicker.

SILK OR CHIFFON. Spread a thin layer of paste on a sheet of glass. Lay a sheet of chiffon, about an inch larger in all directions than the sheet to be treated, on the pasted glass. Give this sheet another coat of paste and lay the paper on it, using the paste brush to smooth it down and ensure complete contact. Give it another coat of paste, and then lay on the second sheet of chiffon, carefully smoothing it down with the brush. Next strip all three sheets from the glass, an easy and simple task for the experienced hand but not so lightly undertaken by the beginner. However, if previous warnings have been followed, the first trial at this sort of work will be with material of no great importance, and it will call for no great amount of effort before one begins to get confidence and to handle the wet, sticky sheets with ease and assurance. Hang the sheet on a rack, frame, or line already provided. When it is half dry, place it between wax boards, put it into press for half an hour, strip the sheets from the wax boards, put them between new wax boards till fully dry, and then press them once more, overnight or for several hours. When dry the overhanging edges of silk should be trimmed even with the paper to prevent unsightly fraying.

If there is much mounting or patching to be done it may perhaps be best to finish that part before beginning to paste the entire sheet. Slight repairs may be made while the sheet is on the pasted glass before the final sheet of silk is laid down. There is danger here, however, that the paste may dry and spoil the job. Here again experience must be the teacher.

JAPANESE TISSUE PAPER. The process is about the same when using Japanese tissue, except that pasted sheets are hung up to dry instead of being placed between wax boards and blotters. For this, wooden spring-clip clothespins may well be employed. The sheets are pressed when fully dry, and ironed at low heat or run through a heated mangle to press them still further and to make them as smooth as possible.

OTHER TRANSPARENT MATERIALS. Here again the development of synthetic materials offers possibilities which overcome shortcomings found in traditional materials. Not all have lived up to the hopes they once offered, however. Cellophane, though it has been used in the absence of more suitable materials, is not to be recommended, since its own chemical structure—representing only a 75 per cent alpha cellulose content—is sometimes less stable than the paper on which it has been used.

Other synthetic materials used for treating irreplaceable documents have given rise to doubts as to their probable permanence, howsoever useful they may be for other purposes. Pressure-sensitive adhesive tapes, based on plastic sheeting, have been developed which, unlike those first introduced, do not disintegrate or turn yellow. Thus "Demco-Seal," "Permafilm," and "Plastic-Kleer" have found acceptance by some librarians, both in tape and wide- (12-inch) roll form. Yet it is perhaps better to think of their use as patching rather than repair, suitable only for materials destined for temporary usefulness. And though they may be employed on tears in paper, their use on leather can still not be advocated, since it is virtually impossible to remove them from bindings without damaging the leather.

LAMINATION. On the other hand, cellulose acetate foil both in use and under severe tests has proven itself. Various refinements of the lamination process employing it have been worked out since its large-scale introduction at the National Archives in Washington. Originally designed for the preservation of vast quantities of archival materials, it is not without interest for librarians whose demands are not as voluminous. In contrast to silk and Japanese tissue, where the paste attracts insects, cellulose acetate foil has the added advantage of protection against them.

The basic process in lamination is to make a sandwich: of tissue, cellulose acetate foil in sheets (1 millimeter in thickness), the leaf to be treated, foil, and then tissue. The sandwich is then submitted to heat and pressure, the result being a sheet the thickness of which is not unduly greater than the original. Heat and pressure are supplied at the same time in the massive laminating machine developed at the National Archives, by means of a steam-heated flat-bed hydraulic press. Its cumbrous size makes its use feasible only for institutions operating on an extensive scale. With the less complicated machine developed by William Barrow of the Virginia State Library of Richmond, the sandwich is first placed between electrically heated platens and then submitted to pressure between cylinder rolls. At the Istituto di Patologia del Libro in Rome, a small-scale, electrically operated, flat-bed press has been developed which, while avoiding the size of the Archives machine, accomplishes the task in a single operation, while that of Barrow requires two steps.

Other smaller machines have been designed for the use of business firms seeking to preserve records. The reliability of these machines is as yet unproven since they unfortunately have not been submitted to the tests conducted by Wilson and Forshee at the National Bureau of Standards which are reported in their recent *Preservation of Documents by Lamination*. It should also be pointed out that Wilson and Forshee recognize that not all acetate foils are of equal quality, and they set forth specifications. Although archivists and others have resisted the use of lamination, Wilson and Forshee's study should go far to dispel misgivings entertained about it.

DE-ACIDIFICATION. Another process introduced by Barrow gives greater value to the lamination process, that of de-acidifying the document before laminating it, a step likewise recommended by Wilson and Forshee, who found that acid in paper also affected the foil itself. De-acidifying is beneficial not only to papers to be laminated but for those which are not.

The process first developed by Barrow called for soaking the document in a saturated solution of limewater (i.e., 0.15 per cent calcium hydroxide) for 20 minutes, and then placing it in a solution of 2 per cent calcium bicarbonate for an equal length of time. More recently Barrow has evolved a single-step process. This calls for a solution "prepared by passing carbon dioxide for two hours through a solution containing 1.5 to 2 grams of calcium carbonate and 15 to 20 grams of magnesium in 1 liter of water. Nearly half of the magnesium carbonate and about one-tenth of the calcium carbonate is converted to bicarbonates. After the undissolved particles settle, the clear solution is decanted for use. Papers to be de-acidified are soaked in it overnight." (*Science*, April 24, 1959, p. 1080.)

Here again the university librarian may call upon his chemistry department to manufacture the solution; others may find it worth while to call upon the industrial chemist to provide it.

The importance of this solution extends beyond its use for materials to be laminated, for it can properly be used for other papers with dangerously high acidity; it was, in fact, with this use in view that Barrow developed it. Whether or not book publishers will utilize this method of protecting book papers, as envisaged by Barrow, remains to be seen.

LAMINATION BY HAND. As for using the lamination process itself, with a machine such as that of the National Archives or Barrow's smaller but still expensive one, few librarians will feel justified in undertaking so extreme a step.

A simpler process using cellulose acetate foil which has been worked out by the National Archives of India is described by Goel and by Kathpalia. Materials treated by this method compare favorably with machine-treated documents under standard tests for longevity and strength.

The document to be treated is placed on a smooth glass surface. Over it a sheet of cellulose acetate foil, cut to provide a margin, is placed, and then Japanese tissue. With a lint-free cloth, acetone is applied to the tissue paper, beginning in the center and moving outward, thus dissolving the acetate foil and binding document and tissue together. When this process is completed, and the surface is dry, the document is turned over and the other side treated in the same manner. The resulting sandwich is then trimmed with scissors, leaving a small margin in the sides. The results are improved if the sandwich is placed in a book press for several hours. It must be borne in mind that acetone is slightly toxic, and that such work with it must be done in a well ventilated room.

DELAMINATION. Not the least of the advantages of cellulose acetate sheeting is that, if for any reason it is found desirable to remove the foil, this can be done by soaking it with acetone.

LOOSE LEAVES. Loose leaves may be inserted in a book in several ways. One is to lay the leaf flat on the table alongside the book. Cover it with a sheet of waste stock, except about one-eighth of an inch along the inside margin. Hold the covering sheet carefully and run the paste brush along the margin; the covering sheet will prevent the paste spreading over the page. Lift the waste sheet and place the sheet for insertion inside the book so that the pasted edge will adhere to the adjoining leaf in the book. Protect the pasted portion by waxed paper and press the book till dry.

If the page to be inserted threatens to project beyond the fore edge when finished, the obvious remedy is to cut off the projecting part. A better plan is to fold the inner margin slightly, say about one-eighth of an inch, paste the turned-over part, insert, and press. This has the advantage of using the fold as a hinge, which is, however, dangerous and inadvisable if the paper stock is brittle, weak, or poor, alas all too often true. In such a case it will be best to cut the leaf and bind it to the stub by means of a paper hinge or thin cloth.

REPAIRING CORNERS. With a page that has been dog-eared and lost a corner, try to get a sheet of paper of the same stock, weight, color as the remaining portion. Lay it under the sheet and with a pencil lightly trace on it the outline of the missing part. Then tear it in a way to give a corner with two straight edges and an inside edge roughly following the pencil line, this corner to have its inside edge about one-eighth of an inch farther from the outside than the pencil line; the torn part should show an irregular bevel or feather edge. Paste the bevel edge, lay it on the corner, protect the sheets with wax paper, put the book to press, and trim with scissors when dry.

FILLING HOLES. If a page has had a hole torn in it, losing a picture or part of the text, for instance, the ideal is to replace it by a perfect copy of the same page from a book otherwise imperfect—unless you are dealing with an early or rare book where such "sophistication" can be bibliographically misleading to scholars not aware of the substitution. If no replacement page can be found, the hole may be filled by a "window" of onion skin or bond paper. Take a sheet of this kind of paper, lightly mark on it the outline of the tear, bevel the edge of the original page and of the replacement sheet, paste, join, protect with wax paper, and press. The window or inlay thus made will prevent further tearing as the page is turned.

LOOSE COVERS. Sometimes new books, fresh from the publisher, show loose covers. Perhaps the paste dried in the machine, and the book went through before the fact was noticed. Perhaps it fell on its edges, or perhaps it was opened roughly

or was bent too much in the middle. Open the volume carefully and spring the hollow back of the cover away from the
"bone" of the book. If there is space enough, use a long, thin
brush to apply paste or polyvinyl acetate emulsion. If the opening is too narrow for this, get a knitting or crochet needle to
carry the paste or acetate to the parts that need it. Close the
volume, rub the back with a bone folder, and put it away to
dry.

HINGES AND JOINTS. It is at the hinge or joint that a
book gets most wear and strain. Every time it is opened, friction and tension are set up in the hinge. The basis of the hinge
or joint is the material connecting the body of the book with
the covers. Formerly the book was sewed to cords that were
laced into the covers, and it was these cords that were flexed
every time the back or covers were opened or closed. Not so
long ago came the discovery that manufacturing costs would
be lessened and manufacturing time would be speeded if book
and covers were connected by means of thin cloth, called super,
glued first to the bone of the book and then to the insides of
the cover boards. This strip of super is ordinarily about as long
as the book is high, and is wide enough to project about half
an inch or a full inch beyond each side of the back. It has but
little strength, is thinner and more frail and fragile than cheese-
cloth, and pleads eloquently for care and attention when the
book is handled. If to this weakness and thinness weak or brittle
glue is added, it is plain to the blind that expectation of life
is short.

RECASING. When this super gives way and the book breaks
from its cover, the usual thing to do is recasing unless complete rebinding is necessary. The first step is removal of all
cloth, paste, glue from the back. The sewing should be examined to see that it is intact. The end papers should be stitched
on the back and front. Take a piece of medium-weight canton
flannel or muslin as long as the book is tall and two inches
wider than the back. Paste this to the back, which has just

been given a coat of flexible glue or polyvinyl acetate emulsion. The cloth, if properly put on, will extend one inch on both sides of the back. It must then be rubbed down smooth and firm with a bone folder, and be put aside till dry. End papers and projecting pieces of cloth must be trimmed flush with the book. Lay the book in its case, open the front cover, paste the end paper, close, and open the back cover, pasting the other end paper; close the book, put it between boards, and into a press until dry. To prevent the end papers from sticking to each other, insert wax paper at both front and back before putting the book to press. This recasing is a pretty piece of work when done by a competent hand. Sober old age advises, however, that cheap and unimportant volumes be used for experimenting.

LOOSE BACKS. The preceding is all well enough for present-day "trade" books, but if the volume has a modern loose or spring back different methods must be followed. A tube or loose back must be made by folding back on itself several times a strip of strong kraft paper, just as long as the book and wide enough for three folds. First cover the back with glue or polyvinyl emulsion, and lay this strip of paper on it with the edge of the paper along one edge of the back. Rub it down smooth. Fold the paper back on itself and run a narrow—that is, perhaps a quarter inch—line of glue along the exposed edge of the sheet as glued to the book. Use this glue to fasten the part of the paper just folded back to the edge of the sheet first glued to the back. Then fold the sheet back once more, this time along the original edge, glueing this folding to the sheet. You thus have one part of the sheet glued to the back, another part folded back on this first part and free except at the fold and the edge where the two are glued together. Cut off any part of the sheet that projects. Open the free part with a bone folder, and you have the foundation for your hollow back. It is not quite so complicated as it reads, and if you watch a binder do it once you will have no difficulty in following him.

And now for the back. Glue a strip of cambric or muslin two inches wider than the back to the outside of the thrice-folded strip of paper. Then paste the new leather back to the cloth, and you will have a loose back on the book instead of a tight back.

TIGHT BACKS. Tight backs are usually found on old books; loose backs generally mark more recent bindings. A tight back is stronger than a loose back, but it cannot be used with clothbound books, because the flexing as the book opens cracks and creases cloth, whereas leather in good condition is supple and flexes easily. A thin volume on thin paper will do better with a tight back, and conversely a thick one on thick paper with a loose back.

REBACKING. Sometimes the call comes for rebacking and rebinding, usually in the case of books of special interest for any one of a dozen reasons. Little more is called for than experience and skill on the part of the binder, two things easy to ask for but less easy to secure. If he knows his business he will remove the original cloth, the end papers too if necessary, though this adds to the difficulty. The signatures may then be resewed if need be, or individual sheets repaired, as the case may require. New backing is then applied, new boards or covers provided, and the old cloth and end papers pasted to the boards.

Scholarly purposes as well as sentiment sometimes call for the use of as much of the original cover as possible, even if parts are worn or broken. In such a case the volume is re-backed or rebound, as much of the old cover replaced as is consistent with protection, and the vacant spots merely proclaim that a piece of honest restoration has been done. A good piece of craftsmanship deserves praise so long as no attempt at deception has been made. In the proper circumstances repairing books is commendable, straightforward restoration is praiseworthy, but work of this kind done to fool the unwary speaks for itself.

WEAKENED OR BROKEN HINGES. Frequently the pared portions of leather bindings begin to crack at their hinges and the sides of the book threaten to come loose. Rather than re-back the volume, the hinges may be restored or strengthened by the use of a polyvinyl acetate emulsion. For this it should be employed at full strength as supplied in emulsion form, and carefully applied with a brush. In doing so the greatest possible caution should be exercised that the emulsion not come in contact with the paper of the end leaves or of the book; it may be well to lay a sheet of wax paper not only between the cover and the end papers but between the end leaves and the first and last page of the book as well, since the emulsion may seep through the cracks onto the body of the book as printed. At full strength the emulsion should be applied only to portions where the leather has given way completely. After the emulsion has been applied it may be allowed to dry briefly, but then the book should be wrapped in wax paper and the portions treated held together by pressure, by elastic bands, or by cords. One's tyro efforts in using the emulsion should be made on books of little value as one learns for oneself the limitations and the merits of this product. Its amazing elasticity and strength justify its use where more laborious measures are uneconomic.

SAVING ORIGINAL LEATHER BACKS. If you have a book bound in leather, and for one reason or another wish to save the old leather on the back and sides, you may replace the worn leather at the hinge with new, rather than use an acetate emulsion. Or you may find the old leather so far gone as to make it impossible to use it, but you want it replaced new on back and at the hinge.

In such a case the old leather must be taken off as carefully as possible. If the book has a loose back the problem is simpler than if the leather is glued tight to the back. It likewise is simpler if the volume is comparatively modern than if it is one of the old-fashioned type with signatures sewed to raised cords or bands. Lift off the old leather with a thin, flat knife, and set it aside for future use if fortune favors and permits removal entire with no breaks or tears. Sometimes the leather is so old and brittle that breakage is inevitable, but sentiment or other considerations call for its return to the volume. It is then removed in pieces as large as possible, which are set aside for reassembling later and pasting on the back.

The leather is now all off the back or bone of the book. Next comes the work on the leather on the boards or sides. This is lifted up with a thin, flat knife if there is any danger of breaking the skin by use of the ordinary bone folder. At this time it may be well to lift up the portions of the end leaves that cover the turnover part of the leather. Moistening the end sheets will soften them and permit their being turned or lifted up without harm.

And now for the replacement. A piece of new leather should be chosen, as near the old in color and texture as possible, two inches wider and one inch taller than the old back. Pare its edges, a little more at top and bottom than along the side. Then give it a coat of paste or polyvinyl emulsion, and fasten it to the back of the book. It is needless to remind the reader that the book should already have been thoroughly cleansed of all paste, glue, and leather. Brush paste into the slits of the boards from which the old leather was taken, and then insert the sides of the new leather, working them under the old leather left on the boards but lifted carefully by the knife or bone folder, as was just mentioned. Now turn in the top and bottom of the new leather, working them under the end leaves.

Rub all joints smooth with a folder, place wax boards or sheets of wax paper between the end leaves and the boards, put the book to press until it is thoroughly dry. If the paper along the inside joint has been torn or worn it may be necessary to paste a strip of similar stock along the joint, keeping the book open while these strips are drying.

Then carefully paste the old back to the new if it was removed without tearing, or match the pieces of the old leather back and paste them down in a way to make them match and give the original appearance. For this your polyvinyl acetate may again prove more workable than a flour paste. Rub the back down and put the book to press for final drying. After it is taken out comes the time for inspection of new leather at the joints. If the shade matches nicely, well and good. If not, then comes a session with brush and pot of stain to make new and old live together in peace and harmony.

INTERLEAVING. Interleaving prevents much wear and tear to the material it protects, provided the paper used is acid-free: if it is not, more harm than good may be done. As a first step toward interleaving paste a strip of thin, strong paper, preferably Japanese vellum, along one side, using a strip about an inch and a half wide and two inches longer or higher than the piece to be protected. This makes a stub or hinge. Treat in this way all the pieces to be handled, and then lay them between sheets of durable paper at least one inch larger, top and bottom, and on both right and left sides, than the largest of the pieces to be protected. If the interleaving is done with single sheets, they must be oversewed; but if it is done with sheets folded into sections, they may be sewed through the fold and bound like any other book. This protection will undoubtedly lengthen the life of many specimens, and will permit the book to be opened without danger of harm when it is laid flat for photographing or for exhibition.

This is all very well when the materials being interleaved are all of the same size. Less is to be said for the practice of mounting materials on blank leaves and binding them up in a volume, as is often done with autograph collections, ephemera of various kinds, and the like, when they are irregular in shape or bulk. Inevitably there will be gaps between the blank leaves at the top of the volume, and where dust is prevalent it is all too likely to seep down between the leaves. The materials mounted are, moreover, not particularly protected from theft, since it is comparatively easy to detach them from the blank leaves, although the frequency with which libraries are asked to photostat or microfilm their manuscript materials makes the demounting process a tedious one. The storage of manuscript materials in manila folders, either flat, or with support vertically, in manuscript boxes, is perhaps to be preferred. Boxes are now manufactured without paste and glue and may be confidently recommended. The "Fibredex" boxes manufactured by the Hollinger Corporation of Arlington, Virginia, may be cited.

LABELS, PAPER OR LEATHER. Labels sometimes have their lettering marred or scratched off. They may be replaced by new ones after the remains of the old have been carefully removed by means of a knife or scraper. New labels should be cut from paper or leather. Paper offers less difficulty than leather, as the leather must be washed with a size of thin paste to make it take the marking ink properly. Lettering using India ink should be put on the label and be perfectly dry before the label is fastened, with paste or polyvinyl acetate, on the book. When it is safely dry and fast on the book, it may be gone over with a protecting coat of thin book varnish or lacquer.

"PERFECT" BINDINGS. The development of the so-called "perfect" bindings for books has been one of the most remarkable publishing phenomena of recent years, although the idea goes back to the nineteenth century when rubber-based adhesives were unsuccessfully used. Their development is due in our day to the polyvinyl acetate adhesives. Such books are characterized by not having their folded sheets sewn together; instead the folds of the sheets at the spine are shaved, treated in one of several possible methods with polyvinyl acetate, usually under heat, and then cased with paper wrappers or even cloth bindings.

While the durability of the adhesive is remarkable, occasionally it will break down, the leaves coming loose. Individual leaves may be restored by applying a narrow strip of slightly thinned emulsion to the inside edge, but from time to time it may be necessary to treat the entire spine. With paperbacks this can be done by removing first the cover and then the earlier acetate adhesive. Placing the volume in a finishing press, if one is available, facilitates removing the acetate. Acetone may be used, or the acetate may be rubbed off with emery paper, or the spine may be carefully shaved with a binder's plough. Then a fresh coat of polyvinyl emulsion at full strength may be applied, and the cover replaced. Adhesion will be improved if the volume is wrapped in wax paper and then held together by pressure. S. M. Cockerell recommends supplying new end papers, sticking a strip of muslin an inch and a half wider than the book over the spine and new end papers, adding a strip of kraft paper over the muslin, and then recasing the book by pasting down the new end papers to the cover.

WATER-SOAKED BOOKS. With books, water is an excellent servant but a most harmful and dangerous master. It is used at many stages of the manufacture of paper, and the stock retains its affinity for water through almost its entire life. When paper is made into books, however, water is one of its greatest enemies. Warped covers, swollen and stained, pages wrinkled and creased mark the afterlife of the book exposed to water. Heavily sized paper, coated with starch or glue or clay, is ruined by contact with water. The size, softened by the water, causes the pages to stick to one another, and if they dry in this state the book is a solid mass. Try to separate the pages, and the surface coating—and print—pulls off from the center, and the only destination for the volume is fireplace or waste pile. Books made of better paper will stand wetting with less serious damage, but their pages inevitably wrinkle and swell distressingly. This may be helped by dampening a few pages at a time with a moist sponge, smoothing down the wrinkles and creases, putting the pages between dry blotters, and allowing them to dry under pressure. Repeat with a few more pages till the whole volume has been treated.

If a book has been thoroughly soaked it will probably be best to take it apart, smooth out the single leaves, drying them under pressure, and then collate and bind it once more. When this must be done, the paper will probably need resizing, as described on page 68. Paper in contact with water will nearly always be stained. Most of this staining will be removed in the sizing bath, but when sheets are not sized the stain may frequently be removed by use of soap and water applied with a soft sponge. In work of this kind undamaged papers must be protected by wax paper or blotters.

DAMAGE BY FIRE. Books damaged by fire offer various problems. If the covers are charred and the boards intact, scrape off the char from the covers and paste a new outer cover over the boards. In some cases it may be best to take the old cloth off entirely and recase the volume. If just the edges are charred, put the book in a finishing press or vise, scrape the edges clean with a steel scraper, and then use sandpaper to get a smooth surface. Gilding or marbling will probably remove all traces of the accident. If the margins permit trimming, take the book out of the cover, trim top, bottom, and fore edges with hand or power cutter, and then recase it.

If the text has been damaged and it is worth the expense, the charred edges may be trimmed off to uniform size and each leaf be inlaid, the whole then being sewed and rebound. Or it may seem best to remove the char, fill in damaged spots with fresh paper, mount each page between silk or tissue paper, or laminate it, and then rebind. If damage has been limited to but a few pages, take them from the book, repair, and then insert on stubs left for the purpose.

When fire has made the paper so brittle that handling becomes difficult, the sheet may be sprayed with a solution of gelatin size. The size should be hot, driven through a hand or power sprayer, and may be made according to the instructions on page 68. Sheets so treated should be covered with silk or tissue paper, or with acetate foil.

INK REMOVAL. The best ink remover is frequently a sharp steel eraser or scratcher, wielded by a skillful and competent hand. If the ink has penetrated too deeply into the paper for removal by this means try the commercial ink eradicators obtainable at any stationery dealer's. They are usually two liquids, one an acid and the other chlorine of lime. The latter added to the acid gives off free chlorine which bleaches the chemicals in the ink. They should be used as sparingly as possible because of their possible aftereffects upon paper: an honest blot is better than a gaping hole in the paper.

India ink of the waterproof variety yields to none of the chemical removers. If the steel eraser cannot scrape it away, better give a sigh and cover the spot, if need be, with a sheet of paper pasted over it.

WHITE INK REMOVAL. White lettering ink is soluble in water. It is used for lettering dark-colored surfaces. Libraries often use it for indicating class marks, call numbers, authors, and various other things on the backs or sides of books, sometimes protecting the entry by a coat of varnish or white shellac. Alcohol will remove the varnish, and water can then be applied to the ink. This is all well enough for the removal of the ink, but with the ordinary book cloths alcohol and water soften the filler of the cloth and start the colors running. If there is danger of this, better try the steel eraser.

PITCH, TAR, AND WAX STAINS. Mutilation or disfigurement by pitch or tar is fortunately not frequent in books. It does happen now and then, and the steel eraser is the first resort. After as much as possible has been removed by this means, try turpentine for the next step. Be careful to see that the tar does not dissolve when the turpentine is applied, and spread to do more damage: a supply of clean cotton wool should be quickly available. After the tar has been thoroughly softened by the turpentine, and the page seems clean, wash the sheet carefully with benzene. Wax should likewise be first scraped with the steel scratcher. Then wash it with benzene, applied with a swab of cotton wool. This does not apply to sealing wax, which is proof against every chemical that will not harm the paper. The steel eraser or scraper is the only hope in such a case.

SOLANDER OR SLIP CASES. Every now and then a book calls for treatment on account of its binding or cover. Sometimes a pamphlet must be cared for without binding, or the owner may wish to keep the unsullied sheets just as they came from the press or folder. More and more discriminating collectors prefer retaining an original or contemporary binding, however battered, to having a book rebound. For all of these some sort of case may need to be made.

Of the varieties which have been designed by binders of the past, a solander case gives the best protection for bindings. This takes its name from the eighteenth-century Swedish botanist who became keeper of the Natural History Department in the British Museum and developed this form of protection. The solander case furnishes complete covering for the volume, stands upright on the shelves, is divided into two parts, the lower one with a neck over which the upper one fits. The cover should fit the book rather snugly, and the leather should be about the same in quality, color, and finish as that of the volume to be protected. Sometimes the case is lined with flannel to prevent scratching the binding. This is one of the most expensive cases to be made, as well as one of the most satisfactory so far as protection is concerned.

There are many other forms of slip covers, cases, boxes, jackets, wrappers, all to be made out of paper, cloth, or leather; the last three are listed in order of increasing cost and amount of protection afforded. Satisfactory making of a cover of this kind is a pretty test of the skill and judgment of a binder. The amateur can give himself much amusement and instruction by trying to make covers out of binder's boards, using paper or cloth for decorative finish.

Sometimes the binder is confronted with a book printed on paper of such poor quality as to defy sewing or any other form of binding, yet of such importance as to call for preservation in this form. In such cases life may be lengthened, if not immortality assured, by making a box, with hinged or slip cover or sides, of fitting size to hold the volume and to permit its standing upright with little further harm. This box may be covered with paper, cloth, or leather, the selection of material being dependent on the binding of related volumes or the value and importance of the material thus protected.

SUPPLY HOUSES. Many of the materials mentioned here may be purchased from library supply and bookbinding supply houses. Attention is called, moreover, to the annual "Buying Guide" for library materials published in *The Library Journal* for April 1 each year. Paper, small cutlery, and paste may be carried by a local stationer or art supply house. Chemicals and oils can be got from or through the local chemist or druggist. The "Yellow pages" of one's local telephone directory, or of that of the closest large city, will list under "Adhesives," "Cellophane (and other Cellulose) Materials and Products," "Chemicals," "Lacquers," "Laminating Equipment and Supplies" other materials not available through the library supply houses. Reference may also be made to *Thomas's Register of American Manufacturers.*

Of library supply houses, the following may be mentioned:

Bro-Dart Industries, 56 Earl Street, Newark 5, New Jersey.
Demco Library Supplies, Madison 1, Wisconsin; New Haven 2, Connecticut.
Gaylord Brothers, Inc., Syracuse, New York; Stockton, California.
Remington Rand, Inc., Library Bureau Division, 315 Park Avenue South, New York 10, New York.

Of the houses mentioned, the first three publish manuals for the repair of book materials, employing, understandably enough, the materials they offer for sale. That the adhesive cloths, mending tapes, etc., recommended have a place where permanence is not the object is perhaps true, but they may also be viewed as time- and money-saving expedients which are inappropriate for treating valuable materials.

For paper the Nelson-Whitehead Paper Corporation, 7 Laight St., New York 13, N.Y., may be recommended. Attention is also called to the wide variety of materials useful to librarians, ranging from papers of all kinds to binding tools and supplies, available from Dryad Handicrafts, Ltd., of Leicester, England. Such materials may be imported by libraries without duty, and may be paid for by checks drawn in dollars on one's local bank. A catalog is available.

Mr. Willman Spawn, of the American Philosophical Society, recommends the inexpensive heavy neutral paper (for packing, etc.) manufactured by the Union Paper Mills, of New Hope, Pennsylvania.

Chapter Five

THE TREATMENT
OF PAPER, VELLUM,
ETC.

TREATMENT OF THE PAPER STOCK. The treatment of the paper stock is usually the first requirement in the repair or reconditioning of manuscripts or old books. Sometimes, to be sure, it may be the binding or cover, the ink, or the pigment in illumination or decoration that needs attention, but the chances are in favor of the paper's requiring aid and treatment first of all. If the paper is unbound and in the form of loose leaves, the methods of treatment and handling will be practically the same as in Chapter 4, except that more patience, skill, care, and attention must be given. If the paper needing repair or mending is a few leaves in a bound volume, a skilled workman may be able to handle them without rebinding the volume completely, but there is no doubt that better work can be done if the book can be taken out of its covers and the sheets handled flat.

PAPER FOR MENDING. With the risk of the charge of repetition fully in mind, let it be said that the same general principles govern here as in Chapter 4. Mending paper should

63

be of the same grade, thickness, and texture as the page to be repaired, or as near as possible. Any binder or restorer with a plant of any age will usually have stored away a quantity of loose sheets of old paper of all sorts, held for just such uses as this. Thickness, weight, texture come first as specifications to be met. They are less simple to change than color and tint. With the first three granted or assured, it is usually fairly simple to meet the problem of color or tint. Darkening may be secured in various ways, but if bleaching is undertaken, restoring a normal hue is complicated. With a solution of tea or coffee an experienced workman can darken a sheet to almost any tint desired. If you watch him at work you will notice that he first tries a sample bit or full sheet and gets it thoroughly dry before he steeps the working sheet. It is dangerous to accept a solution unless one has tested it under working conditions and is sure of the result, whether a solution of tea or a solution of a problem.

ETHICS OF REPAIR WORK. Just when it is right to repair a tear or make a restoration so completely as to show no signs of repair or restoration is a question of ethics that must be passed on for each individual case. There is no general rule governing all instances. If the end and aim are deception, then the effort is indefensible. If it is merely an effort to return the page or sheet as nearly to its original condition as possible, then the effort may be commendable. It all depends on the aim in view. Some collectors and booklovers insist on the repair and restoration being performed in a way to render the page perfect but to show in plain and honest fashion just what has been done. Scrupulous restorers often annotate the piece treated, explaining what has been done and dating the work. Repair is honest; deceit is not.

FILLING HOLES IN PAPER. Several varieties of Japanese tissue are suitable for mending torn pages. Pages with large tears, holes, missing parts may require extensive patching. Worm holes and similar perforations from any other causes may be filled in by means of a paste filler made of paper pulp or paper fluff and paste. This pulp or fluff may be got by scraping a sheet of the same paper stock with a sharp knife, scraping fluff from blotting paper, or reducing paper to pulp by boiling paper cut up in fine fragments. Add the paste to the pulp and stain the mixture, if need be, to match the stock to be repaired. Spread the original sheet out on a piece of plate glass, dampen it and fill the holes with the pulp, applying it with the blade of a small knife, smoothing it with a bone folder or similar instrument, placing it between wax boards for drying in a press.

CLEANING PAPER. When it comes to a question of cleaning paper, remember that the first qualifications are good common sense, added to a knowledge of paper stock. Before beginning to clean paper a prudent workman will make a careful appraisal to see how strong it is and how successfully it will probably withstand the rigors of cleaning. It is a really wise man who knows when to let well enough alone. Even a soft eraser may be too much for some weak-fibered and brittle stocks.

RUBBER ERASERS. If the paper is reasonably strong, several methods of cleaning lie open to choice, depending largely on the nature of the spots to be removed. Surface dirt, pencil and finger marks, soil that has stained the surface but not penetrated deep will frequently yield to a soft rubber eraser, a sponge rubber, a piece of art gum, even a small lump of day-old bread or clean dough.

A few spots in a bound volume may be treated here and there, but if there are many it is better to take the book out of its binding. Recasing may call for more care and attention, but the result will probably be better if the sheets can be handled freely and be put to press by themselves, leaving those that need no treatment to rest in peace. But by taking the book out of its binding one is able to undertake treatment which is not feasible otherwise.

WASHING OF PAPER. Good rag papers and many others may be cleaned by one means or another, but not only must the character and strength of the paper itself be considered but the nature of the text it carries. Ordinary printing inks may usually be washed without hazard, and so may some writings inks, such as those of oak gall origin, or India ink (if care is taken not to rub it from the surface). The prudent workman will test the material to be handled by applying a tiny drop of water to an inconspicuous part of the text; by touching a white blotter to the spot he can tell whether the print or writing is likely to come off.

In many cases, water by itself—which should be distilled, if possible—will do much to clean paper, freeing it of dust and grime and restoring some of the life it has lost if dry and brittle. It will also remove at least some of the acidity where this is present. Sheets of paper which can be handled in this way may be slipped carefully into a tray of water, such as a photographer's developing tray. Rocking the tray will loosen much of the surface dirt, or a camel's hair brush may be carefully used.

Materials which it seems better not to submit to immersion may be sponged, with water or a soap jelly. Take care to see that the soap is pure, free from scent or coloring materials; a good castile soap is best.

Papers which have been thoroughly washed will probably need to be resized, as described on page 68. The exacting rare book collector prefers his books not to be washed and resized, but here again each case must be judged on its merits. Coated paper, highly glazed, should never be touched by water, which will certainly dissolve the surface and ruin the paper beyond the possibility of repair.

SOLVENTS. For stains of a more permanent nature, solvents may be used, though they must be used cautiously, and never near an open flame. Their fumes may be ignited several yards from any flame. After using them open the windows and change the air. Solvents may also dissolve not only the stains but the printing ink as well, causing it to run and give another and unexpected stain.

Benzene, benzole, and gasolene are particularly helpful in removing oil and grease stains. Saturate the spot with one of these solvents, place the sheet between blotters, and go over it with a hot iron, hot enough to remove the stain but not hot enough to burn the paper. If the stain is old and saturation heavy it may be well to soak the spot thoroughly in kerosene for several hours before using the benzene, benzole, or gasolene. Alcohol is excellent for removing iodine, mold, and mildew stains.

For these and other types of stains the National Archives in Washington provides the following table:

Stain	Recommended Solvent
Adhesive tape	Carbon tetrachloride or benzene
Duco cement	Acetone
Glue (linen or glassine tape)	Warm water
Lacquer	Acetone
Oil	Carbon tetrachloride or benzene
Paint	Mixture of alcohol and benzene
Paste	Water
Rubber cement	Mixture of benzene and toluene
Scotch tape	Mixture of benzene and toluene
Shellac	Ethyl alcohol
Wax	Mixture of benzene and toluene

In using these solvents the National Archives recommends that "The paper itself should be laid with the stained side down on a white blotter and the solvent should be sponged on from the back. . . . As the solvent is applied successively, the paper should be moved to clean portions of the blotter. When repeated sponging leaves no significant residue on the blotter, the paper should be turned over and treated in a similar way on the stained side. After the solvent has dried, no ironing or other flattening treatment should be required." (Minogue, 1943, p. 23.)

SIZING OF PAPER. Most papers, except blotting paper and soft, high-bulking book stock, are sized. Sometimes sizing is done in the beater before the paper is made, but in the better grade papers sizing is done after the sheet has taken shape. Size is normally any gelatinous substance, such as casein or starch or glue, that is added to the paper stock to glaze the surface, adding to the strength, and permitting the use of ink which otherwise would spread. With book and writing papers it is usually a good quality animal glue. Put a sheet of paper in a bath of water, or treat it with chemicals, to wash or bleach it, and you will find that removing the stain or discoloration or dirt has likewise removed the original sizing. The sheet is limp and soft, useless for its original purpose.

RESIZING. But resizing will restore it. This, however, should be the last step in the process of restoration. All other things must have been cared for, nothing remain to be done but to return the surface to its original condition. To make the size, take one ounce of the best gelatin or of isinglass and dissolve it in 32 ounces of water. Mild heating of the water will hasten the process. Reducing the amount of water will make the size stronger, but the heat should be applied gradually to prevent danger of burning the liquid and turning it brown.

If luck or skill has been with you there will be a clear liquid in the container. Strain this through a clean cloth into a shallow pan large enough to hold the sheets about to be treated. Best results will follow if this shallow pan can rest above a gas flame, electric plate, or some other form of heat to keep its contents at about 125 degrees Fahrenheit.

And now comes the time for immersing the paper. But be sure to look at it carefully once more, to be certain it calls for no further attention, to be sure all dirt and pencil marks and finger prints have been removed. If not, sizing merely means fixing them. Some stains, however, will be removed in the warm bath, especially brown water stains.

Carefully slide the sheet into the size bath, and then take it out, not too slowly, not too hastily. Put the sheets on top of one another. When the whole book has been treated, the pile of sheets should be placed between backing boards and put in a backing or finishing press to have the surplus liquid squeezed out into a pan placed below to catch the drip.

Then spread the sheets out on large, clean sheets of paper to dry. It means that care must be taken to prevent the sheets from sticking together while in the press or while laid out to dry. With proper equipment it may be best to clip each sheet to a line and let it dry, hanging in the air at a convenient height. Or the joined leaves of a book may be placed at their fold over a line. In any event, dust and dirt must be kept from the sheets. After drying they must be run through a mangle or press, then folded and made ready for binding. If there are only a few sheets for treatment, it may be sufficient to lay them between sheets of clean blotting paper, then ironing or pressing them when dry. But in all cases be sure that they are quite dry before taking the next step, whatever that may be: of recasing, rebinding, or mounting, or filing in manila folders.

FOXING. Not infrequently on old paper, less commonly in modern stocks, one finds a dull rusty patch discoloring the page in annoying fashion. This comes from "foxing," the term going back to the rusty red of Reynard the Fox. The fullest research on this problem has been done by T. D. Beckwith and Thomas M. Iiams, who find that foxing is caused by the growth of fungi. The foxed areas are more acid than the unfoxed or clean parts. Paper-infesting fungi can produce acid in a medium in which cellulose is the sole source of carbon for this acid by-product. Starch sizing increases acid, casein decreases it, rosin seems to inhibit both the growth of fungi and the production of acid.

Iron in paper—a result of chemical impurities unremoved during the process of manufacture—stimulates the growth of fungi, which in turn is responsible for the development of by-products rich in insoluble iron salts that are not only injurious to paper fiber but productive of the characteristic "fox" color as well. These reactions are to a certain extent dependent on the amount of moisture present.

Paper weakened by improper methods of manufacture, by excessive variations in humidity, by unintelligent use, tends to be favorable to the growth of foxing. Storage in steel stacks in fairly well-ventilated rooms, where the moisture content does not exceed 75 per cent of saturation—or, best of all, in air-conditioned quarters—helps much to reduce foxing.

Although Beckwith and Iiams were unable themselves to recommend a solution for the problem of foxing, the use of thymol crystals, as described above on page 31, is now the accepted treatment; and what was said there in terms of molds and mildews can be applied to foxing in paper. Chloramine T, described further on, may also be used to remove the discoloration.

BLEACHING. The bleaching of paper for the removal of stains may be done by several chemicals, all with the advantages and disadvantages of such treatment. The fly in the ointment appears in the shape of the warning that many chemicals remove spots and also weaken the paper. Bleaching is perfectly possible, but it is recommended only when it will not do more harm than good. There will, in fact, be few occasions when it is really necessary for books, far fewer than with the treatment of prints, drawings, engravings, and similar art objects. Fortunately, earlier methods employing potassium permanganate and potassium metasulphate have given way to others which are both simpler and safer, if less potent.

BLEACHING WITH CHLORAMINE *T.* The least difficult of all agents to apply, dispensing as it does with trays and repeated washings, chloramine T is mild in action. A white powder, it is used in a 2 per cent solution, that is, with 4 ounces of powder to 5 quarts of water (or in proportion). The solution is painted with a fine, flat brush on the surface to be cleaned. The leaf treated should then be put between blotting paper and boards and pressed, under weights or in a book press. If after an hour the stain has not disappeared, the treatment may be repeated until a satisfactory appearance is achieved. Chloramine T as well as thymol may be used for the treatment of foxing. When not in use, the powder should be kept in an airtight bottle, since it is an unstable compound and will disintegrate on contact with air.

SODIUM CHLORITE. Another method, developed by R. J. Gettens, though less simple, has many advocates. Here a 2 per cent solution of sodium chlorite is used (that is, 4 ounces to 5 quarts of water), to which is added 5 ounces of 40 per cent formaldehyde. The material to be bleached is submerged in a tray containing the solution—another use for our photographer's developing tray—and then washed in running water. How long the material should be kept in the solution will vary with the intensity of the staining: a 15-minute period is suggested, and an equal length of time in running water. Needless to say not all paper will be strong enough to submit to such handling. After such treatment, the material should be dried between blotters and pressed as in other methods.

OTHER FORMULAS. Many other formulas have been brought forward, some with a record of success and some with less fortunate histories. Several which have won approval in museum practice are described in detail by M. C. Bradley,

Jr., in his *Treatment of Pictures* (1950). Oxalic acid, javelle water (chlorinated potash), ammonia, hydrogen peroxide, sulphite of soda, bicarbonate of soda, and other solutions and combinations all have their advocates, but too often they offer danger of failure or destruction unless one brings to the effort satisfactory training in chemistry.

DANGERS OF WEAKENING. Bear in mind also that this attack by chemicals, this washing and rewashing, this bleaching may be safe with paper of undoubted strength, but it is weakening even for the best, and certainly is dangerous for stocks with fibers affected by attacks of one kind or another. The experienced eye will decide not infrequently that it will be more satisfactory to accept the sheet with the stain and with a known and certain strength rather than to succeed in removing the stain and at the same time bring about dangerous weakening of the fibers. Occasionally decay has gone so far that covering with silk, Japanese tissue, or acetate foil offers the only hope of preservation even with the stain left in all its rawness.

TREATMENT OF COLOR PRINTS. Remember too that treatment of black-and-white prints (whether made by ordinary typography or by engraving or etching processes) is one thing and treatment of color prints decidedly another. Color prints made with ordinary fast colors, aquatints, modern offset color prints, and all ordinary black letter prints and engravings may be treated with every hope of success if the washing or bleaching is done with ordinary care and attention. Such prints may be cleaned and brightened, may have all traces of stains removed from the paper without damage to the color.

But danger lies in the face of the man trying to treat in this way paper bearing colors, or sheets printed with ink of fugitive colors, or sheets with highly coated surfaces. The water colors will run, the fugitive colored inks will disappear or bleach. Starch and clay and size of the highly coated surfaces will soften and stick together or the surface coating will wash off completely as soon as the sheet is given its water bath. Even with black-and-white prints a knowledge of ink and color is advisable. Bleaching tends to weaken ink and color and paper stock. Modern carbon inks are acidproof, to be sure, but even with them there is constant and insistent call for attention and alertness. An open mind and a willingness to experiment will well repay all efforts they demand. In case of doubt or question it is surely simple to find a piece of paper similar to if not identical with the one in question, and test and try it before giving the primary sheet its irrevocable plunge. When only a small portion of the sheet is liable to danger, it is possible to cut out a piece of cellulose acetate foil and lay it over the danger zone, applying acetone to it with a swab of cotton wool. After the treatment of the sheet has been completed, the foil may be removed by further application of the acetone.

RESTORING LETTERING. Sometimes the printed page suffers an accident that dims the text by rubbing, chemical action, or various other causes. Restoration is not impossible for the steady hand guided by an experienced eye. The obvious means is a bottle of India ink and a draftsman's pen. It is difficult at this point not to recommend to the craftsman that he acquire some practice if not skill in calligraphy as an adjunct to his efforts in restoration.

Printing types may also be used. For this latter process select a face as near the original as possible. Spread a bit of printer's ink on a sheet of glass or other smooth surface, by means of a brayer or printer's hand-inking roller. Dampen the paper slightly. Ink the type by means of the brayer, getting on not too much or too little. Then press the type down on the paper. Two or three "warming up" exercises on specimens where mistakes are not vital will help ensure success on the important sheet where an error is unforgivable. Be sure, however, to experiment with a sheet of the same general character as the original stock.

RESTORATION OF RUBRICATED LETTERS. Restoration of faded rubricated initials is possible by means of ink of proper shade and material; for this the information contained in the relevant chapters in *The Calligrapher's Handbook,* edited by C. M. Lamb, will be helpful. Or a good oil paint applied by a fine camel's hair brush will often give satisfaction. The treated pages should dry thoroughly before being handled. Rubrication or illumination done by oil paint or by printer's ink necessarily calls for oil color or printer's ink restoration; where the decoration is in wash or water colors restoration must be in the same medium. It is surely needless to sound a warning against letting anyone but an artist and workman of unquestioned ability undertake a task of this kind.

VELLUM AND PARCHMENT. Parchment and vellum present decided difficulties in handling. Made from the skin of calves or sheep, they change almost as rapidly and widely as the thermometer. That statement is exaggerated, as a matter of fact, but there is no doubt about the trouble they make while kept under modern conditions.

PREPARATION OF SKIN FOR WRITING. Skin has been used for writing materials from an early date. It comes down to us usually in the form of a volume or codex, sometimes also as the binding of such a volume, more rarely in the primitive form of a roll. The skin was limed, washed, stretched, scraped, rubbed smooth with pumice stone, and then turned over to the scribe. Skins from stillborn calves were usually selected for the finer sheets. Those from the older animals were usually so tough they could be put to better use as bindings than as sheets for the written message.

Vellum in any form is affected by heat and moisture more than paper. It is inclined to stretch, shrink, wrinkle, cockle, warp as the surrounding air grows more or less moist or humid. This explains the straps or thongs or clasps found so frequently on old parchment bindings. But even such fastenings fail to keep the cover flat and straight, and for shelving under modern conditions better results will follow the use of a slipcase than of thongs or clasps. The case should be tight enough to keep the volume under constant pressure, loose enough to permit the book to be put into it or taken out without harm.

BLEACHING VELLUM. Old vellum is frequently yellow or cream in tint, sometimes just cream enough to be altogether attractive, but not infrequently so near brown as to render the writing difficult to read. It may be bleached, but bleaching, even with chloramine T, should be chosen only as a last resort, the burden of recommendation for such action being serious and demanding unquestionable justification. What such justification may be it is difficult to imagine. The danger of making the ink or colors run is something to be borne in mind, for most specimens calling for attention will probably be manuscripts done with writing inks rather than printed pages, and some writing inks are less permanent than most printing inks.

CLEANING VELLUM. Far better first to try to clean the sheet, by sponging with a lather made from a good soap, free from acid or alkali, the lather made with as little water as possible. After sponging carefully, wipe it dry It may be put into a book press, between blotters, which should be changed as they become moist, with a minimum of pressure; but it is better to lay the sheet flat, on blotters, and to hold it taut while drying by weights at the edges. A soft rubber eraser, alcohol, and benzene are other cleaning means to fall back on as need arises.

SMOOTHING WRINKLED VELLUM. When it comes to straightening vellum leaves that have bent or twisted or cockled, the first thing to do is to moisten them; but real care must be taken to see that water does not come into direct contact with the sheet. This is particularly important in the case of illuminated manuscripts. Water may be applied directly, to be sure, but there is danger then of starting the ink to run or even danger of removing it. A safer way is to apply this moisture by means of a humidifier or a box made in a way to hold moistening pans or to permit the safe introduction of steam.

STRAIGHTENING SINGLE SHEETS OF VELLUM. If the book can be taken apart the problem is simpler than if it must be met by treating the bound volume. With single sheets it is simple to make a frame of wood, slightly larger than the sheets to be treated. Then attach clips (if of metal, covering the surface with masking tape or sticking plaster lest rusting occur), with strings attached to weights. The sheet can be so adjusted that there will be an even pull in all directions and the moisture will permit it to be flattened evenly. Be sure that it is completely dry before removing the clips and strings. The drying should be gradual, and sometimes (where otherwise mold might develop) it may be well to apply artificial heat if the heat can be kept well under control. But haste will do more damage than good here. Remember that parchment originally came from Pergamum in the East, and remember the word of advice about trying to hurry the East. It holds good here without question.

Sometimes vellum may be softened by the application of steam, but live steam must never come in contact with the skin.

Be sure that the sheet is perfectly dry when taken from the press. Otherwise you have the work to do all over again, for warping and cockling are almost inevitable unless the drying was complete.

OIL FOR VELLUM. After the vellum has been washed with soap and water it will be somewhat softer, and before it becomes brittle and hard again it should be given two or three applications of a leather dressing, rubbed well into the skin. The dressing may be either one of neat's foot oil and lanolin or others discussed in Chapter 6 for application to leather.

This will keep the skin in good condition and help render it less affected by moisture or dryness in the air.

WARPED VELLUM COVERS. Pasting an extra sheet of paper inside each cover often helps to correct badly warped vellum covers. This tends to draw the covers inward, and to keep the boards flat by counteracting the outward pull of the vellum.

BOARDS. Wooden boards were first used in early books. It is obvious that when replacement of such boards becomes necessary the same type of wood should be selected, if possible, that it should be dry and thoroughly seasoned to prevent warping. Wood, covered with leather or paper, was also used by early American binders, especially in New England, when they were unable to secure paper boards for one reason or another. But after the invention of printing from movable types, wooden boards were largely supplanted by paper boards made from sheets of printers' waste pasted together. Later on the increased demand brought about the manufacture of binder's board made from old rags, rope, and waste paper. Boards have been made for special and selected books from many materials such as cork, plywood, bakelite, metals, fiber, and plastics. All of these have had one drawback or another, none of them proving as satisfactory for normal book production as a good quality, solid binder's board.

OTHER LEATHER MANUSCRIPTS. Manuscripts on leather that is decidedly neither vellum nor parchment sometimes come to attention in the shape of drawings on skins made by American Indians or other primitive peoples. They need about the same kind of treatment as other skins, moistening to flatten with pressure, application of a dressing to keep them soft and pliable, the sewing of tears to prevent further running, or patching with fresh skins to fill holes or straighten edges. Skins as nearly the color and texture of the original should be chosen, to make an obvious remark, the edges shaved as the piece is cut to the size of the hole to be filled, the binding being done by means of a good leather cement or with polyvinyl acetate.

Need for care of this kind will come so seldom to the librarian or collector or binder that attention to individual cases may well be left to the specialist or the museum expert when the need arises. But, to repeat once more, the same general principles governing attention to vellum and parchment and leather bindings will govern here.

PAPYRUS. Papyrus is the name applied to the writing material used by the ancient Egyptians, the Greeks, and the Romans. It was prepared by cutting longitudinal strips of fibers from the papyrus plant, laying them across one another at right angles in two layers, soaking them in water, and pressing them into a smooth, even surface. There was enough natural glutinous matter in the fibers to cause them to adhere closely when pressed or beaten dry; some people credited this adhesion to the peculiar qualities of the water of the Nile. After they came from the press they were smoothed with pumice stone or some other abrasive.

The ink used on them was probably made from water, glue, lampblack, or carbon. This must constantly be borne in mind, as there is danger of seeing the ink run if the sheet is carelessly soaked in water.

PAPYRUS SHEETS. Papyrus sheets come in various sizes and in all sorts of conditions. They were usually made into rolls about twenty or thirty feet long, but sometimes were used as single sheets about the size of one's palm. They come to us today in both forms; to meet modern conditions the rolls should be cut into convenient sections and these sections, as well as single isolated sheets, should be protected by glass.

STRAIGHTENING PAPYRUS SHEETS. Many of these sheets are sadly wrinkled and creased, brittle and dry, breaking at the slightest attempt to flex or bend or fold. The first requirements for straightening them and putting them into condition for reading are skilled hands, intelligent eyes, common sense, and an alert mind. To these immaterial things may be added such equipment as a sheet of plate glass, some sponges, a tray for water, some small brushes, blotters, flat-bladed knives, and at least one knife with a pointed blade.

First see that the sheet of glass is absolutely clean: when rubbed down with distilled water, no drops will adhere to it. Then wash it off with benzene. This will leave a slight film of oil on the glass, preventing adhesion. Now dampen it with a sponge and water. Spread a piece of fine silk gauze smoothly over the glass. Put the papyrus on the gauze and wet it with a sponge and water until it becomes soft and flexible. Flatten out the wrinkles by stretching and pressing. The point of the knife or a small brush may help rearrange fibers that were fixed discouragingly out of place. Turning back portions folded over may occasionally bring the thrill of revealing part of the text hitherto hidden and unknown.

More water will bring out dried mud and dirt, but this water must be removed quickly by soaking it up with the sponge. When the necessary folding and flattening and smoothing have been finished, blot off the surplus water, and lift the sheet off the glass by means of the silk gauze, which will thus support the papyrus and make removal more safe and easy than without it.

Put the papyrus down on a blotter and strip off the gauze. Let it dry partially and then put it to press. If pressed while it is too wet there is danger of blotting off the ink. If the papyrus is allowed to get too dry before pressing it will wrinkle and cockle again.

When both sides of the sheet bear writing two glasses may be used, both prepared in the same manner with benzene and gauze. Finish the first side of the papyrus sheet, strip the sheet off the glass, lay it face down on the second sheet of gauze and glass. After it has been treated, washed, flattened, finished, strip it and place it on a blotter for drying.

When dry the sheet should be perfectly flat, but it will not stay flat unless it is protected, something best secured by laying it between two sheets of glass and binding them together by a cloth tape, a glass adhesive, or a wooden frame. If there is no writing on the back, or no other objection, it may be well to mount the papyrus on a good quality of picture mount board and frame it under glass. Sometimes it may call for covering with silk before putting it under glass.

In all this it is experience and common sense that ensure success much more than any formal set of rules to govern details of method and procedure. A binder competent to do work of this kind will succeed if he is grounded in the fundamental principles of his work and supplements them by an alert mind and an active interest in accomplishing the unusual, no matter whether he has been given rules or not. No need to tell him to try his first ideas on pieces that do not count rather than begin with an attack on papyrus of first importance.

ORIENTAL MANUSCRIPTS. Manuscripts from the farther East, China, Japan, Nepal, and India, appear on paper, palm leaves, birchbark, and occasionally on leather. Treatment of the paper stock is governed by the same principles controlling paper made in the western world; earlier specimens are all handmade and are usually better than the machine-made samples of more recent years, or even than the handmade papers made today by village craftsmen in India. In fact, in India one encounters early manuscripts, repaired in recent times with modern paper, where the latter, frequently a wood pulp paper made from bamboo, within a matter of a few years has turned brown and will soon disintegrate.

Techniques of handling such materials differ only as the foundation stock differs from more common paper. So too with writing on birchbark, where silking is practiced with some success. Leather is leather, even when written on, and its care and treatment are essentially the same whether it was tanned or prepared east of the 180th meridian or west of it.

PALM LEAF MANUSCRIPTS. Manuscripts on palm leaves demand treatment rather infrequently in the West, but in the East they still occur in vast accumulations, such as those of the Saraswati Mahal Library of the rajas of Tanjore, or the universities of Madras and Mysore. Like paper and leather, palm leaves are liable to all the ailments caused by the extremes of climatic conditions in the tropics: humidity, heat, insects, and mildew. To fill the holes in them resulting from insect attack is perhaps more a matter for the cabinetmaker skilled in veneer work than for the binder, but if such repair is at all called for it may be done by using plastic wood, tinted to a matching color. For cracks and fractures once again we may call upon polyvinyl acetate. The best prevention against damage is air conditioning, but brushing the leaves with an aqueous solution of zinc chloride or sodium fluoride should offer some protection. Unfortunately much work remains to be done in the study of the problems of palm leaf materials. In the West, where so much of our basic research on preservation has been undertaken, palm leaf manuscripts are too rare to call for the investigation given to paper and to leather.

Manuscripts from the Pacific Islands call for such special attention as to insist on treatment and care by workmen of special skill and experience who need no help from a book such as this. Each case must be handled as its demands are studied. Holes must be filled by something as nearly like the original as possible. Tears must be controlled by some safe adhesive. Protection must be assured by restoring the covering wrapper, by making a new frame, by taking such steps as the case seems to call for. If the workman is intelligent and skilled and honest he will know at what stage he must call for help and advice. If he is not of this type the work should not be put into his hands.

Chapter Six

THE CARE OF
LEATHER BINDINGS

Leather as a binding material. Of all bookbinding materials leather comes nearest to being ideal. It is pliable, can be worked to advantage by both forwarder and finisher, takes tooling and gold admirably, is good to look upon, is delightful to handle. Till recently it was the most lasting material known for this purpose, and was always specified when books were to be bound in the best manner possible.

MODERN TANNING. The tanner, however, yielded in the nineteenth century to the insistent cry of the customer for more speedy delivery, and for more spectacular leather finishes. He renounced the time-honored traditional methods, used sulphuric acids to secure brighter hues, rushed the hides through the vats, and handed the binder a skin inferior in every way—save quickness of tanning—to those produced with less haste and more conservative methods.

Early in this century the problem of leathers which had been produced in the second half of the nineteenth century evoked investigations in England. In this country the binders of the New York Public Library also realized how conflicting were the pieces of information and advice they were able to secure as to treatment of leather, and they set out to experiment and observe for themselves. Every solution or preparation that came to attention or could be found by diligent search was tried, and careful notes were taken of the results. Samples for testing were selected from levant, morocco, pigskin, calf, cow, sheep, tanned in this country and in England, France, and Germany. Swatches from designated parts of each hide were exposed to gas light and gas fumes in a chamber specially constructed for the purpose. Some were exposed to sunlight and to air under glass, and others to direct sunlight and the usual city air. Some were treated with various preservatives and some were left untreated.

The experiments continued for many months, each particular exposure being at least 2,500 hours. At the end all the samples, treated and untreated, exposed and unexposed, were sent to the Bureau of Standards in Washington. Study and examination there showed that all skins treated with any approved preparation were benefited, even those which had been acid-tanned. Chrome-tanned leathers withstood gas fumes better than those treated with vegetable tanning, though as a method of tanning book leathers chrome tanning has not won acceptance.

The general experiment showed conclusively that acid-tanned leather deteriorated when exposed to heat and to gas-laden air, while acid-free leather suffered less. This experiment on the part of the New York Public Library is confirmed by experiments conducted in England, where is was found that vegetable-tanned leathers are to be preferred to those in which acid has been used in the tanning process.

GAS-CHARGED AIR. It is scarcely fair, however, to lay all the blame for the deterioration of leather on the tanning process. The tanner certainly has much to answer for, but he might very properly ask if the most unmitigated optimist could expect well-tanned skins to overcome the gas-charged atmosphere of our modern cities. There is no doubt that the high sulphuric acid content of the typical industrial city has much responsibility for the decay of leather bindings. If the skin is subjected to dampness the danger of mildew is always present as well. Direct sunlight is harmful also, as is storage in rooms too warm and too dry. The binder cannot escape unscathed if he wet the leather too much or stretched it too much when covering his boards, or if the finisher used oxalic acid or vinegar.

AIR CONDITIONING. But of all the enemies of well-tanned leather sulphuric acid is the most harmful, and must be re-moved from the air or from contact with books. For this, air conditioning is surely the most effective method, and in using it we solve many of the other problems of leather bindings. In this connection, it may be stressed again that the air-con-ditioning process should wash the air with alkaline water, for ‘the electrostatic filters of air-purification devices, while adequate for dust, are not effective against sulphuric gases.

PROTECTION WITH POTASSIUM LACTATE. For the library which has not yet installed air conditioning to ward off the effects of gases in the air, against which even stable vegetable-tanned leathers are not immune, H. J. Plenderleith, of the British Museum, recommends that such vegetable-tanned bindings be treated with a 7 per cent aqueous solution of potassium lactate, after washing them with soap and water and allowing them to dry. (If for reasons of cleanliness the books are washed again later, a second treatment with the potassium lactate will be necessary.) Such a solution may be made up by a chemist in large quantities, and decanted into smaller bottles for use as needed. For protection against mold and mildew, paranitrophenol (0.25 per cent) may be added to the solution.

Although Plenderleith and his associates have found in England that treatment of such vegetable-tanned leathers with potassium lactate was so successful as to make any other treat-ment unnecessary, and oiling them largely a matter of giving bindings an attractive gloss, this perhaps says more about the temperature and humidity of English libraries than about the value of such treatment.

LEATHER DRESSINGS. For this reason, especially in American homes and libraries where hot dry air is for a substantial part of the year all too common, the application of certain dressings may lessen the harmful effects on leather bindings. Some of these dressings are mentioned below. How often they should be applied will depend on circumstances and the rate of evaporation of the oils in question. There is no general and universal rule of faith and practice, but a moderate amount of attention joined to a bit of common sense will soon show when leather begins to dry out, to crack at the edges or hinges from dryness. Of course the remedy should be applied before necessity arises, but it is given to few of us to be foresighted enough to anticipate trouble of this kind. The instructions given by the late Mr. Apley to his son John that the books in the family library be treated with lanolin once a month was characteristically overcautious, and in general it may be safe to suggest once a year or thereabouts for the ordinary collection in the modern building in the average American city. When conditions change to extreme north or south, to very damp or very dry places, the needs must be assessed in terms of local situations by the exercise of individual judgment.

LANOLIN AND OIL DRESSINGS. It may be said that almost any treatment is better than none at all, and it may also be admitted that styles and preferences in dressings change from decade to decade. Numerous formulas for their preparation have from time to time been advanced, and all have their merits, ranging from ease in assembling to the glossiness imparted to the leather.

High on the list of acceptable preparations is that now employed by the New York Public Library, where it has supplanted one comprising simply two parts of lanolin to three parts of neat's-foot oil. It is made up as follows:

Per Cent

	Per Cent
Neat's-foot oil, 20 per cent cold test, pure	25
Lanolin, anhydrous	17.5
Japan wax, pure	10
Sodium stearate, powdered	2.5
Water, distilled	45

The Japan wax is used to give body to the mixture, while the sodium stearate provides a cleansing agent. To prepare the dressing, melt together in a double boiler all the ingredients except the sodium stearate and the distilled water. In another dish mix the sodium stearate and the water; cover the dish and heat until the stearate is dissolved. Then pour the sodium stearate solution gradually into the melted grease, stirring vigorously at the same time. Cool the mixture, which thickens as it cools. Continue to stir vigorously to prevent the separation of the mixture till it is the consistency of a smooth, whitish cream paste. Keep the paste in tightly capped glass jars. The skill acquired in such preparation can be happily applied at home also in preparing sauces for the gourmet.

Other formulas recommended by the United States Department of Agriculture in its leaflet 398, *Leather Bookbindings: How to Preserve Them* (1956), include the following:

	Per Cent
Castor oil, U. S. proof	12
Lanolin, anhydrous	30
Japan wax, pure	5
Sodium stearate, powdered	3
Water, distilled	50

The preparation of the dressing is the same as in that given above.

Two other preparations also employing sodium stearate follow, and are made in the same fashion. In both, heat together all the ingredients till all except the sodium stearate have melted. Pour the result onto a sheet of plate glass, and as it cools knead the lumps of sodium stearate into the mass until it is evenly distributed.

		Per Cent
(A)	Neat's-foot oil	35
	Lanolin, anhydrous	50
	Japan wax, pure	10
	Sodium stearate, powdered	5

		Per Cent
(B)	Sperm oil, winter strained	25
	Lanolin, anhydrous	55
	Japan wax, pure	15
	Sodium stearate, powdered	5

Perhaps the simplest of all dressings is that consisting simply of 3 parts of neat's-foot oil with 2 parts of lanolin. The lanolin is heated in a double boiler; when it has melted, the neat's-foot oil is added and stirred until the mixture is even in consistency. It is more liquid than those described above, and lacks their cleaning action.

DRESSINGS FOR VELLUM. Of the dressings described above, those embodying water and neat's-foot oil and lanolin preparations have been effectively used on vellum. The sodium stearate will provide some cleaning action, but one must not expect to remove the yellowish tints of many skins. Very little dressing will need to be applied, since it is not absorbed by the vellum.

APPLICATION OF DRESSINGS. Whatever the mixture selected, it may be applied with a flat varnish brush of convenient size, or, preferably, with a soft cloth or pad which permits the user to work the preparation more effectively into the pores of the leather. An excess of the dressing should not be allowed to stand in creases of the leather, and gilt lettering should be touched as little as possible. Let the books stand for a few hours or overnight until the oil is absorbed. When dry, rub and polish with a soft cloth. If a higher gloss is desired, apply a small quantity of castor oil with a soft cloth or pad, and when it is dry rub the surface with a chamois or sheep's wool polisher.

Take care to keep the oil away from the paper edges of the book or from the cloth used in some bindings. Experienced workers frequently hold the book in the left hand and apply oil and cloths with the right. It is certainly needless to remark that large volumes should be placed firmly on the table and should receive particular attention to see that no unexpected mishaps mark the treatment.

Newly bound books may be treated on receipt, with a second treatment six months later, and a third in about a year if conditions seem normal and average.

BRITISH MUSEUM DRESSING. Despite Plenderleith's limited faith in the utility of leather dressings, the British Museum continues to make use of one in which lanolin serves as a lubricant, to which wax is added to consolidate the leather where there has been superficial decay. The formula is as follows:

Lanolin, anhydrous	7	oz. (by weight)
Beeswax	.5	oz. "
Cedarwood oil	1	oz. (by volume)
Hexane	11	oz. "

Dissolve the wax in the hexane in a warm place, taking care to keep it away from naked lights, as hexane is volatile and easily inflammable. Add the cedarwood oil, and then lanolin, which should be previously softened by warming. The mixture must be thoroughly shaken before using.

"The chief reasons for combining these ingredients in this leather dressing may be briefly stated as follows. Lanolin is an animal fat which is very easily absorbed by leather and does not become rancid. At ordinary temperatures it is in the form of a thick grease, and to use it thus would be to get uneven results and unduly strain the leather binding. A little wax is added to assist in polishing and to provide a thin surface film which, in the treated binding, reinforces any powdery or cracked portions of the leather and provides a protective 'skin' of considerable importance, particularly in the case of vellum bindings. The cedarwood oil, in addition to its well-known qualities as a preservative, is of value in forming a bond of union between the lanolin and wax in the leather, and hexane is chosen as a convenient 'thinner' as it readily dissolves beeswax.

"The method of applying the mixture is as follows: First the bindings are washed in the usual manner [with soap and water], and set out to dry in a warm room for two or three days, and then the leather dressing is well rubbed in. The leather will now feel greasy to the touch, but after standing for forty-eight hours it will be found that the lanolin has penetrated and the binding can be easily polished. This operation leaves a shiny 'skin' on the surface which shows the grain of the leather to the best advantage. It is not in any way a sticky or resinous surface after polishing, and the general effect of the treatment is to soften the leather and prevent it from drying up.

"This mixture forms a very cheap and effective dressing for all kinds of leather and vellum." (*British Museum Quarterly*, 2, 1927, 77-8.)

SECRET PREPARATIONS. From time to time other formulas have been brought forward, and these need not be disregarded. Some are described as secret preparations, so carefully compounded as to urge the fortunate discoverer to keep the mystery sealed from curious or unsympathetic or unappreciative eyes. The temptation is strong to ask if you have sufficient ground for confidence that when the seer was granted insight into the mysteries assurance was also given that no harmful ingredient was thoughtlessly or inadvertently added. *Caveat emptor.*

Some of these "secret" preparations have been analyzed and found to contain harmless ingredients, but they have been priced much higher than the component parts could have been bought for in the open market. Of course the seller deserves remuneration for time and trouble in combining the materials, in providing attractive packaging, and in evolving an enticing name, but whether the cost is justified may be left as a matter of opinion. Common sense asks why one should choose a "secret" formula when harmless and helpful ingredients lie freely at hand.

READY-MADE DRESSINGS. For those who wish to purchase the leather dressings already prepared, antiquarian and rare book dealers frequently offer such preparations for sale, generally made up from specified and acceptable formulas.

MINERAL OIL AND LEATHER. Vaseline and other mineral oil compounds have their earnest advocates, but some of us believe that the less mineral oils are used on leather the better it is for the leather. Ask any machinist what effect mineral oil has on leather driving belts, and he will tell you that it causes the belt to crack and disintegrate, in direct contrast to the effect of animal or vegetable oils. Bookbinders will generally give the same testimony as to the relative effects of animal and vegetable oils as contrasted with mineral oils, so far as leather bindings are concerned.

TREATMENT WITH LACQUERS, ETC. Few bookmen are happy at having their leather bindings in anything but what may be called a "natural" state, the leather oiled to preserve it, yes, but without any further treatment that alters its pleasant feel or surface. This would be all very well if all leathers were sound, and all had received in their lifetime the care and consideration necessary to preserve them. But not infrequently leather bindings call for acts of desperation—treatment with plastics or with lacquers—to keep them from uselessness or complete disintegration.

POLYVINYL ACETATE. In such circumstances one may have recourse to a polyvinyl emulsion. Not at its full strength, but thinned down with water in accordance with the instructions furnished by the dealer in the particular brand used, varying probably from three to five times the strength of the emulsion as sold. Experience alone can direct the choice of concentration.

The solution is applied with a brush, which (need we say again?) should not be allowed to become dry but be dipped frequently into water. Because of its water content, the solution should not be applied to leather which retains a dressed, oily surface. Such a surface should first be sponged with water into which a few drops of solvent, such as carbon tetrachloride, have been stirred.

Polyvinyl acetate has its particular advantages in the treatment of shabby leather bindings. It will solidify the particles of rotted leather which are often present, and make them adhere, and water colors can be added to the solution to achieve a uniform color when needed. Leather dressing can also be applied to the binding after such treatment; it does not leave a hard, glossy surface if the emulsion has been thinned down.

The fact remains that with some bindings the application of the emulsion when diluted with water has its disadvantages. This is particularly true with bindings where thin wooden boards have been employed by the binder, as was frequently the case with early American bindings. The absorption of the water by the boards often causes them to warp. Even putting them to press after treatment (when the emulsion has turned from its whitish hue to a transparent state) is not always sufficient to overcome this tendency.

ACRYLIC RESIN LACQUERS. As an alternative to a poly-vinyl acetate emulsion, lacquers or varnishes may also be used. These are preferable to shellac or varnish, which often leave a pronounced stickiness—although lacquers are not always free of tackiness.

Good book lacquers can be had at any bookbinding or library supply house, or even one's local hardware store, at moderate cost, and in containers of sufficiently varied sizes to suit the needs of any customer. Of the many types available, that embodying acrylic resin is to be preferred. Such varnishes or lacquers can be applied with a small piece of cotton, a brush, or as a spray, either in the form of an aerosol bomb or by means of blowers. Larger libraries may find it desirable and economical to supply their own spray equipment.

It must be borne in mind that once lacquer has been applied little else can be done to the leather itself except to apply further coats of lacquer. Loose particles of leather should be rubbed free first with emery cloth; scuffed portions of leather should be glued down; areas where the surface color has been rubbed away may be stained with matching leather dye. If wished, a final coating of leather dressing may be applied before the lacquer.

The technique employed will vary with the form of lacquer, and the manufacturer's directions should be respected. It is especially important to remember that most lacquers give off vapors which are inflammable, and may explode in the presence of an open flame. At best the fumes are slightly toxic, and fresh air should be supplied, either naturally or by fans.

In spraying books two thin coats are better than one heavy one. In brush application, the lacquer will probably need to be thinned with the solvent appropriate to the particular brand employed. (Library supply houses offer a thinner as a corollary to the lacquers advertised.) As with all lacquer application, the technique is essentially the same: using a full brush, to apply it in a single stroke or two, not brushing the surface back and forth, bearing in mind that the lacquer dries very quickly.

After use, any brush should immediately be put into solvent to keep it from glueing up.

The result of a lacquer treatment will be a highly glossy surface which is unpleasant for many of us. But it is a surface resistant to molds, mildew, and insects, and one which can be washed with soap and water when the need arises. These advantages may well override objections otherwise advanced.

Chapter Seven

THE TREATMENT
OF CLOTH BINDINGS

C OLOR IN BINDINGS. Color has swept the world of
bookbindings in our day just as emphatically as it has taken
hold of the bathroom or kitchen or any other part of the
house. Not so long ago book coverings were uniform and
somber in that uniformity. Here and there a library would
bind one class of books in one color and another in a different
color, but in every case every book in the class was uniform
and sedate. No frivolity in the book stacks. Within a few
short years book covers and book jackets have yielded to this
color advance. Publishers have vied with one another to find
striking and attractive color effects, and the makers of binder's
cloth have been as successful in selling these rainbow-hued
products to the binders for repair work as for original edition
work. And now the librarian may make a choice from brilliant
colors, pastel shades, embossed patterns, cloths with two-tone
effects. The use of aluminum foil has also meant that the
lettering of cases need not be limited to gold or to standard
shades of stamping inks; now we may have the glitter of silver
and bronze as well.

What is more, the new synthetics permit the wider use of
illustrations not only in black and white but also in color on

94

our book covers, both cloth and paper. What once would have been impracticable because the designs would rub off is now made possible by coating the cases with our old friend polyvinyl acetate.

If this new dimension in book production is the product of a highly competitive market—in the field of textbooks and children's literature particularly—we need not be patronizing toward its economic origin. The fact remains that we may benefit from the new opportunities provided for imagination and vitality. It is in fact a perverse and puritannical view which assumes that the text is the only thing that matters in a book, and that excursions into making books physically appealing are irrelevant.

For the librarian the rainbow outburst of color can appear a burden: to maintain the freshness of such bindings may seem more trouble than they are worth. But the librarian need not feel that the book publisher is indifferent to the problem of producing bindings that will retain their attractiveness or will even meet such special situations as mold and mildew (English librarians complain that in this respect American publishers are more considerate than their own).

CONTINUING CHANGE IN BINDING MATERIALS. So rapid are the strides taken by the book industry that what might be said of the moment may not be true a year or two hence. While pyroxylin (a cellulose-nitrate mixture) for a while seemed the most promising material for the impregnation and coating of cloths, improvements in machinery have led to greater interest in the wider use of vinyl both for impregnation of cloth and for coating the cases themselves. Pleasing effects have thus been achieved, even though we have not altogether escaped from artificial leather effects which, apart from their cheapness and their washability, for many of us offend by their pretense at being something they are not. What lies beyond the horizon in the field of binding materials it is impossible to say, yet the prospect is at least an encouraging one.

BOOK JACKETS. In the meantime the librarian is not without resource in meeting the immediate, practical problem of maintaining the life and appeal of cloth bindings as long as possible. The use of plastic jackets to protect and preserve both dust wrapper and binding has every justification. If by providing them a book circulates more often to more people, their purchase is sound economics. Some day, perhaps, the cloth bindings on all books will provide the advantages of a friction-resisting, washable surface, and the visual appeal of an artist-designed dust wrapper: until that time the plastic jacket is one of the librarian's best friends, and deserves an appropriate part in the library's budget. Not only in public libraries, but in others as well: even in Trappist monasteries it is found that books so protected are read in preference to their shabbier neighbors.

As a compromise, some librarians cover their dust jackets with transparent, adhesive, pressure-sensitive sheeting, such as "Celluseal" or "Clearseal," which can then be affixed to the book itself, inside the covers. For a small library this offers better protection than none at all.

RESTORATION OF BOOK CLOTH. For cloth bindings which are not protected by jackets—those which have been retired from active service—it is possible to retard their decline into hoary age and desuetude.

For those which have been soiled by ordinary handling, often a piece of art gum or a soft rubber eraser will prove a great help. Grease spots and deep-seated grime may sometimes be removed by benzene or benzole. But water should not be used on ordinary book cloths unless they have already been treated in some way by varnish or lacquer. Otherwise they will give up finish, filler, and color when water is applied.

Stained or faded book cloth may in turn be restored by application of a water color stain or a size of proper tint. Make it by dissolving a tablespoon of white of egg in a cup of water. Allow twelve hours for compete absorption. To this add a tablespoon of paste, and enough color soluble in water to give the necessary shade. Strain it through a very fine sieve or thin gauze, and then apply it with a small brush or a soft sponge.

BOOK VARNISHES AND LACQUERS. As with leather bindings, it is possible for the librarian to treat cloth bindings with lacquer when they have not already been bound in an impregnated or plastic-surfaced cloth. Where mold, mildew, and insects are a serious problem, such steps go far in the path of wisdom, whatever one's objections to the appearance of such coatings. Each library will have to decide for itself whether or not the advantages of protection by lacquer or varnish are outweighed by what are in part largely esthetic considerations. The lacquer is applied in the same fashion as with leather (p. 92 above). A light coat of lacquer spray will do much to revive the appearance of the cloth, without resulting in an unpleasant sheen.

Where book cloths have frayed, the threads may be made to adhere once more by applying polyvinyl acetate emulsion. When a cloth binding has reached this stage, and complete rebinding is for one reason or another delayed, full coating with lacquer may be advisable.

Chapter Eight

WHEN ALL ELSE FAILS

No TRUE BOOKMAN is altogether happy at the destruction of a book, however hopeless its condition—unless it is to spare himself the anguish caused by such reminders of bibliographic degradation. But all too frequently, and, Barrow leads us to believe, increasingly, there will be books for which known and accepted methods of restoration are either inadequate or hopelessly expensive. When this occurs, we can at least attempt to salvage what we may by preserving the text through one means or another.

At its simplest, this may involve the actual manuscript transcription of the text, as once done in the Middle Ages, and as continues to be done in India today. One needs, however, to be no paleographer to observe that such transcripts will never have the authority or authenticity of the original text themselves, nor may they even have the longevity, when written on inferior wood pulp paper.

MICROFILMS. The development of microcards and of microfilming materials and techniques is too well known in our day to require prolonged description or discussion. The bibliographer may distrust microfilm, the scholar may deplore the discomfort of using it, but it remains at least a possible means of preserving and transmitting printed texts when others

fail. Its use for newspapers is a saving on every score: of binding costs, of shelf space, to say nothing of repair.

PROTECTION OF MICROFILM. The fact remains that putting material on microfilm does not spare one further concern.
For microfilms, like books, need to be given proper care and
attention. Films, even those on cellulose acetate (which has
generally supplanted earlier unstable cellulose nitrate), can
suffer real damage both in use and storage. Dust, heat, and
humidity are harmful to film as well as to paper.

It will come as no surprise then when it is pointed out that
whatever microfilm reader is used, it should be protected from
dust, and be operated with consideration for the film itself.

Air-conditioned storage is as important for microfilms as
it is for books. Dust and dirt in contact with the film can all
too easily scratch it, and under magnification the scratch may
become monstrous. With excessive humidity (that is, as with
books, above 60 per cent relative humidity) there is likelihood
of growth of mold or mildew on the film, and of the rusting
of the spools on which the film is wound.

Excessive dryness, on the other hand, can cause the film to
become brittle and to curl. Acids by contact or from the air
can harm film as well as paper. In other words, although microfilm has the lasting qualities of stable paper itself, like it also
it is subject to external hazards, and cannot be treated with
indifference. Optimum standards of heat and humidity (see
p. 7 above) or, better yet, air conditioning should be provided not only for books but microfilms as well.

XEROGRAPHY. One of the more promising developments
of recent years in the inexpensive reproduction of book materials is Xerography, which provides a printed image less ex-
pensively than the photostat machine.

In the Xerox process an image can be projected onto an
electrostatically charged metal plate from microfilm. When
ink in powdered form is spread on the plate, it adheres to
the image, and a print can be taken with it. By the use of

a "Copyflo" printer, whereby a continuing roll of paper repro-
duces the text from microfilm, a single copy of a work can be
provided at less cost than photostat. The paper is gathered
"Japanese" style on double folds and accordingly may be bulkier
than the original.

Such reproduction has its limitations. Although line cuts
will normally reproduce satisfactorily, the plate will not "hold"
solid areas of illustration. The book to be reproduced should
be filmed, moreover, with a view to its Copyflo printing, avoiding waste in marginal areas, between frames, and the like.

By using a print produced from microfilm through Xerography as master copy for offset reproduction, University Microfilms, Inc., of Ann Arbor, Michigan, assures us that out-of-
print books may be reprinted in small quantities at low prices.
If this indeed proves to be the case, we shall not be without
recourse in preserving the text at least of books—those, particularly, printed on wood pulp paper—for which known
methods of repair offer little hope.

For new developments in the field of microfilming and in
Xerography, one may profitably consult not only library journals
but also *Microcosm,* the house organ issued periodically by
University Microfilms, Inc., leaders in the field of the microfilming of book materials.

Chapter Nine

A LIST OF REFERENCES

THE LIST OF references in this chapter is a selection from
the enormous quantity of writings relating to the care and
repair of books, chosen primarily for its potential usefulness to
the reader. In addition it serves to acknowledge indebtedness
to authors cited, to substantiate statements made in earlier pages
of this book, and to lead the reader to works which will answer
questions that may arise in special circumstances. Many of the
works mentioned, such as those of Barrow, Edith Diehl, and
Alfonso Gallo, include extensive bibliographies which may
serve as guides to further reading.

For those wishing to keep abreast of new developments, the
English *Journal of Documentation* provides summaries of significant articles on care and preservation, as well as reviews
new books in the field. The librarian will also be well advised
to watch for new developments reported in the *American
Archivist*. Nor should the *Indian Archives* be overlooked. Those
who read Italian will find in the *Bollettino* of the Istituto di
Patologia del Libro the one periodical devoted exclusively to
preservation problems.

Attention may also be called to the periodical *Book Production* for discussions of new techniques which may affect the
care of books in libraries. The *Penrose Annual*, published in
London, provides a yearly report on recent developments in
printing and illustration. The monthly section on Book Production in *Publishers' Weekly* should also be consulted.

1. ADAMS, R. G. "Librarians as Enemies of Books." *Library Quarterly*, 7 (1937), 317-31. Also issued separately, and reprinted in John D. Marshall, and others, *Books, Libraries, Librarians* (Hamden, Conn., Shoe String Press, 1955), pp. 5-17. On the sins committed by librarians charged with the safeguarding of our literary and historical past.

2. ALDEN, J. E. "Why Preserve Books?" *Catholic Library World*, 30 (1959) 267-72. An attempt to explore reasons other than the obvious ones for the preservation of books as physical objects.

3. ALMELA MELIÁ, JUAN. *Higiene y terapeutica del libro.* Mexico, D.F., Fondo de Cultura Económica [1956]. 219 p. Illus.

4. BACK, E. A. "Bookworms." Smithsonian Institution, *Annual Report*, 1939, pp. 365-74. Also issued as the Institution's Publication No. 3572.

4A. BARROW, WILLIAM J. *Deterioration of Book Stock; Causes and Remedies;* ed. by Randolph W. Church. Richmond, Va., Virginia State Library, 1959. 70 p. (Virginia State Library Publications, No. 10.) Includes two studies, the first on "Physical Strength of Non-fiction Book Papers, 1900-1949," the second on "The Stabilization of Modern Book Papers." Both spell out the investigations on which Barrow's earlier report (No. 8 below) was based. The work is printed on an experimental wood pulp paper which promises to have a longevity of at least 300 years.

5. ———— *Manuscripts and Documents, Their Deterioration and Restoration.* Charlottesville, Va., University of Virginia Press [1955]. 86 leaves. Reproduced from typescript. A historical analysis of inks and paper, the causes of their decay, and a description of the author's own de-acidification and lamination processes. Contains an extensive bibliography.

6. ———— "Migration of Impurities in Paper." *Archivum*, 3 (1953), 105-8. Warns against the dangers of allowing paper to come in contact with other papers of unstable nature, since acids do indeed migrate; speaks of other harmful substances, such as paper clips, rubber bands, newspaper clippings, photostats, etc.

7. ———— "Restoration Methods." *American Archivist*, 6 (1943), 151-4. A description of Barrow's earlier de-acidification process and of his laminating machine.

8. ———— AND R. C. SPROULL. "Permanence in Book Papers." *Science*, 129 (1959), 1075-84. A very important analysis of the acidity of contemporary book papers, showing that they are likely to deteriorate greatly within a matter of decades; suggests possible method of de-acidification simpler than that used earlier by Barrow.

9. BEACH, R. F., AND W. H. MARTIN. "Union Theological Seminary Air Conditions Its Library." *College and Research Libraries*, 18 (1957), 297-301. Practical experience and conclusions in the air conditioning of an existing library building, of value to the librarian considering such a step.

10. BECKWITH, T. D., AND OTHERS. "Deterioration of Paper: The Cause and Effect of Foxing." University of California at Los Angeles, *Publications in Biological Sciences*, 1 (1940), 299-356.

11. BENJAMIN, MARY A. *Autographs: A Key to Collecting.* New York, R. R. Bowker Co., 1946. xviii, 305 p. Illus. See chapter 13, "Care and Preservation," pp. 241-59.

12. BLADES, WILLIAM. *The Enemies of Books.* Revised and Enlarged by the Author. London, Elliot Stock, 1888. xiii, 165 p. Illus. (The Book-Lover's Library.) Though of little practical value today, a minor classic which has gone through several editions and can be read with sympathetic response by anyone fond of books as artifacts.

13. Bowman, B. C. "Xerography, Possible Solution to the Bad-Paper Problem." *College and Research Libraries, 19* (1958), 185-6. With this it is necessary to read W. R. Hawker (34).

14. Bracey, P., and F. Barlow. "Urea-Formaldehyde Resin as a Vehicle for Semi-Permanent Insecticidal and Fungicidal Coatings on Bookbindings and Bookcases." *Journal of Documentation, 9* (1953), 157-68. Illus. Contains formula for a lacquer developed for use against insects, particularly in the tropics, which has proved effective. However, as the authors later point out at Plenderleith's urging, the lacquer may discolor bindings, and probably should not be used on books themselves.

15. Bradley, Morton C., Jr. *The Treatment of Pictures.* Cambridge, Mass., Art Technology, 1950. Unpaged. See particularly Part V, "The Treatment of Pictures on Paper." Though designed primarily for the specialist in museum work, this volume should be helpful when simpler remedies prove inadequate.

16. Bro-Dart Industries. *Modern Simplified Book Repair.* Newark, N.J., Bro-Dart Industries [195-]. 11 p. Illus. Means of utilizing polyvinyl acetate emulsions, acrylic resin lacquers, and other products.

17. Brown, Lloyd A. *Notes on the Care and Cataloging of Old Maps.* Windham, Conn., Hawthorn House, 1940. 110 p. Illus. Practical suggestions on the shelving of maps.

18. Burchard, John E., and others. *Planning the University Library Building.* Princeton, N.J., Princeton University Press, 1949. xvii, 145 p. Illus. See chapter 5, "Air-Conditioning," pp. 65-83.

19. Burton, J. O., and R. H. Rasch. "The Determination of the Alpha Cellulose Content and Copper Number of Paper." U.S. National Bureau of Standards, *Journal of Research, 6* (1931), 603-19. Also issued as the Bureau's

Research Paper No. 295. Describes one of the laboratory processes for establishing the probable stability of paper.

20. COCKERELL, DOUGLAS. *Bookbinding, and the Care of Books: A Textbook for Bookbinders and Librarians.* 5th ed. London and New York, Pitman [1953]. 345 p. Illus. (Artistic Crafts Series.) An excellent manual for binding books by hand, which also contains suggestions to librarians on standards to be set for workmen.

21. COCKERELL, SYDNEY M. *The Repairing of Books.* London, Sheppard Press [1958]. 110 p. Illus. Written for the English reader; particular attention is given to the problems of rebinding, recasing, and the like, but other useful information is included.

22. DEMCO LIBRARY SUPPLIES. *Demcobind, A Practical Manual of Mending.* Madison, Wisc., Demco Library Supplies [195-]. 64 p. Illus.

23. DIEHL, EDITH. *Bookbinding, Its Background and Technique.* New York, Rinehart, 1946. 2 v. Illus. Vol. 1 comprises a history of the craft; vol. 2 a manual of hand binding. Chapter 20 of vol. 2 (pp. 297-309) discusses briefly methods of repairing bindings and paper. Extensive bibliographies.

24. DONNELLY (R. R.) AND SONS COMPANY. *All the King's Horses.* [Chicago, The Lakeside Press, 1954]. 41 p. Illus. Also published serially in abridged form as H. W. Tribolet's "Arts of Book Repair and Restoration" in *Book Production,* v. 67-8 (1958).

25. EASTMAN KODAK COMPANY. *The Handling, Repair and Storage of 16 mm. Film.* Rochester, N.Y., Eastman Kodak Co. Sales Service Division, 1959. 11 p. (Its Kodak pamphlet No. D-23.) Contains recommendations applicable to microfilm storage.

26. FEIPEL, LOUIS N., AND EARL W. BROWNING. *Library Binding Manual.* Chicago, American Library Association, 1951.

vi, 74 p. Illus. Designed for the administrator rather than the craftsman, sets forth standards for library bindings, and points out quite rightly that repairing, when what is called for is actual rebinding, is a foolish economy.

27. FILLIOZAT, JEAN. "Manuscripts on Birch Bark (Bhurjapa-tra) and Their Preservation." *Indian Archives*, 1 (1947), 102-8.

28. GALLO, ALFONSO. *Patologia e terapia del libro*. Roma, Editrice Raggio [1951]. viii, 254 p. Illus. (Enciclopedia Poligrafica, Ser. 1, No. 3.) A copiously illustrated history of book preservation studies and methods, and a description of the extraordinary work of the Istituto di Patologia del Libro at Rome, of which the author was founder. It is not, however, a practical manual in any sense. Extensive, if sometimes bewildering, bibliographical references.

29. GAYLORD BROTHERS, INC. *Gaylord's Bookcraft. A Complete Manual on Book Repair*. Syracuse, N.Y., Gaylord Brothers, Inc. [ᶜ 1955]. 32 p. Illus.

30. GETTENS, R. J. "The Bleaching of Stained and Discolored Pictures on Paper with Sodium Chlorite and Chlorine Dioxide." *Museum*, 5 (Paris, UNESCO, 1952-5), p. 116.

31. GOEL, O. P. "Repair of Documents with Cellulose Acetate Foils on Small Scale." *Indian Archives*, 7 (1953), 162-5. An earlier description of the process later restated by Kathpalia.

32. GRANT, JULIUS. *Books & Documents; Dating, Permanence and Preservation*. London, Grafton, 1937. xii, 218 p. Illus. An invaluable reference work, especially for the history of the varying types of paper.

33. GUPTA, R. C. "How to Fight White Ants [i.e., termites]." *Indian Archives*, 8 (1954), 121-9. An excellent summary of the problem as encountered in the Far East.

34. HAWKER, W. R. "Developments in Xerography: Copyflo, Electrostatic Prints, and O-P Books." *College and Research Libraries,* 20 (1959), 111-17. Discusses some of the limitations of Xerography, in extension of B. C. Bowman's article cited above.

35. HETHERINGTON, D. C. "Mold Preventive for Bookbindings." *College and Research Libraries,* 7 (1946), 261. Gives formula for a solution embodying thymol for application to bindings to prevent mold. Since it is poisonous and inflammable, and should not touch the skin, its use is questionable.

36. HUBER, L. R. "Materials and Methods in Book Finishing and Repairing." American Library Association *Bulletin,* 49 (1955), 326-30. An appraisal of newer materials developed for the repair of books, such as pressure-sensitive tapes, adhesive cloths, plastic tapes, and the like, which finds in them merits the more conservative will perhaps question.

37. IIAMS, THOMAS M. "Preservation of Rare Books and Manuscripts in the Huntington Library." *Library Quarterly,* 2 (1932), 375-86. Illus. Describes measures adopted for the California climate, including the vacuum fumigation of books against insects.

38. ———— AND T. D. BECKWITH. "Notes on the Causes and Prevention of Foxing in Books." *Library Quarterly,* 5 (1935), 407-18. For a later and more comprehensive statement of the problem, see Beckwith, as cited above.

39. INDIA (REPUBLIC). NATIONAL ARCHIVES. *A Note on the Preservation and Repair of Records.* New Delhi, National Archives of India [1954]. 15 p. A modest but valuable discussion of means of preventing the deterioration of archival materials and of their repair, in terms of a tropical climate. The information is in large part applicable to books as well.

40. INNES, R. FARADAY. *The Deterioration of Vegetable-Tanned Leather on Storage*. [London, 1931]. 15 p. Illus. Reprinted from the *Journal of the International Society of Leather Trades' Chemists* for October 1931.

41. ————"Preservation of Bookbinding Leathers." *Library Association Record*, 52 (1950), 458-61. There is "very strong evidence that pyrophosphate will prevent commercial leather containing iron [from] absorbing sulphur dioxide and building up sulphuric acid."

42. KATHPALIA, Y. P. "Care of Books in the Libraries." *Indian Archives*, 9 (1955), 147-54. Suggestions for a tropical climate.

43. ———— "Hand Lamination with Cellulose Acetate." *American Archivist*, 21 (1958), 271. A simplified method, dispensing with machinery. See also No. 31.

44. KETT, F. J. L. "Insect Pests of Books." *Book Collector*, 5 (1956), 57-62. Illus. On pests encountered in England and their control, but applicable elsewhere.

45. KIMBERLY, ARTHUR E., AND B. W. SCRIBNER. *Summary Report of Bureau of Standards Research on Preservation of Records*. Washington, D.C., U.S. National Bureau of Standards, 1934. 28 p. (Bureau of Standards Miscellaneous Publication No. 144.) A fine introduction to the methods used in the scientific study of the deterioration of book materials.

46. KISHORE, R., AND Y. P. KATHPALIA. "A Note on Dextrine Paste." *Indian Archives*, 9 (1955), 55. Gives recipe, cited above (p. 40), for a flour paste incorporating insecticidal poisons.

47. KREMER, A. W. "Preservation of Wood Pulp Publications." *College and Research Libraries*, 15 (1954), 205-9. Speaks of possible methods, including lamination. Discusses also the possibility of the development of means for transferring print from disintegrating paper to fresh paper (a process

with which Barrow has experimented), which has however in the intervening years not yet become practicable.

48. LAMB, C. M., ED. *The Calligrapher's Handbook.* London, Faber and Faber, [1956]. 252 p. Illus. Though designed for the practicing calligrapher of today, this contains historical material of interest to the preservationist. See also, pp. 199-223, S. M. Cockerell's "The Binding of Manuscripts."

49. LANGWELL, W. H. *The Conservation of Books and Documents.* London and New York, Pitman [1957]. xxii, 114 p. Written by a practicing chemist, of interest for its analysis of the chemical properties of book materials. Some of the suggestions which Langwell offers using newer chemicals are questionable, not yet having been sufficiently tested.

50. LE GEAR, CLARA E. *Maps; Their Care, Repair, and Preservation in Libraries.* Washington, D.C., Library of Congress Division of Maps, 1949. ix, 46 p. Illus.

51. LEHMANN-HAUPT, HELLMUT, ED. *Bookbinding in America; Three Essays.* Portland, Me., Southworth-Anthoensen, 1941. xix, 293 p. Illus. See especially the editor's "On the Rebinding of Old Books" (pp [187]-283). Does not "contain instructions on how to rebind or repair an old volume, but advice as to the best way to get this done."

52. MASON, J. P., AND J. F. MANNING. *The Technology of Plastics and Resins.* New York, Van Nostrand [1945]. vii, 493 p. Illus. See especially the sections on cellulose (pp. 150-62), acrylic resins (pp. 239-59), and polyvinyl acetate (pp. 272-8).

53. MINOGUE, ADELAIDE E. "Physical Care, Repair, and Protection of Manuscripts." *Library Trends,* 5 (1957), 344-51. A summary statement.

54. ——— *The Repair and Preservation of Records.* Washington, D.C., The National Archives, 1943. 56 p. Illus. (The National Archives Bulletin No. 5.) A valuable description

of the rationale and methods of National Archives practice, based upon the widest possible use of scientific principles. The librarian, though his problem may not be archival, will nonetheless profit from the statement of principles.

55. ——— "Treatment of Fire and Water Damaged Records." *American Archivist,* 9 (1946), 17-25.

56. *Miscellanea di scritti vari in memoria di Alfonso Gallo.* Firenze, Olschki, 1956. viii, 711 p. Illus. A memorial volume to the founder of the Istituto di Patologia del Libro, comprising forty essays, partly on preservation, partly historical or bibliographical. Includes discussions of termite control, war-damaged libraries, lamination, etc.

57. MORGANA, MARIO. *Restauro dei libri antichi.* Milano, Hoepli, 1932. xvi, 192 p. Illus. (Manuali Hoepli.) The standard Italian work in the field, now somewhat outdated.

58. "New Trends in Vinyl Binding." *Book Production,* 68 (1958), 40.

59. NEW YORK STATE LIBRARY. LIBRARY EXTENSION DIVISION. *Your Book Collection: Its Care.* Albany, N.Y., New York State Library, 1957. 52 p. Illus. Largely a discussion of how to keep a collection as a whole attractive and inviting, rather than of the care or repair of individual volumes.

60. NOLL, D. F. "The Maintenance of Microfilm Files." *American Archivist,* 13 (1950), 129-34.

61. "Out of Print Books Restored by Xerographic Process." *Book Production,* 68 (Nov. 1958), 68, 75. On the use of Copyflo printing from microfilm.

62. PLENDERLEITH, HAROLD J. *The Conservation of Antiquities and Works of Art.* London and New York, Oxford University Press, 1956. xv, 373 p. Illus. The distillation of a lifetime's research and practice by the world's foremost authority in the field of preservation. Although books

figure in this work only as one of the artifacts bequeathed to us by the past, the volume is indispensable to all concerned with the care of leather and paper in book form.

63. ⸺ *The Conservation of Prints, Drawings, and Manuscripts.* [London and New York] Oxford University Press, 1937. vi, 66 p. Illus.

64. ⸺ *The Preservation of Leather Bookbindings.* London, The British Museum [1950]. 24 p. Illus. First printed in 1947, this pamphlet outlines the causes of decay in leather, both within itself and from the atmosphere, recommends the use of vegetable-tanned leathers and a potassium lactate buffer, and discusses leather dressings, giving the British Museum's formula (cited above, pp. 88-9).

65. ⸺ AND ANTHONY WERNER. "Technical Notes on the Conservation of Documents." *Journal of the Society of Archivists,* 1 (1958), 195-201.

66. PLUMBE, W. J. "Storage and Preservation of Books, Periodicals and Newspapers in Tropical Climates." *UNESCO Bulletin for Libraries,* 12 (1958), 156-62. A Malayan librarian surveys practices employed in the tropics throughout the world. Or see the author's "Preservation of Library Materials in Tropical Countries," *Library Trends,* 8 (1959), 291-306.

67. ROGERS, J. S., AND C. W. BEEBE. *Leather Bookbindings: How to Preserve Them.* Washington, D.C., U.S. Department of Agriculture, 1956. 8 p. Illus. (The Department's Leaflet No. 398.) Supersedes Leaflet No. 69, *Preservation of Leather Bookbindings.* Describes numerous dressings and their merits (some of which are given on pp. 85-8 above), their manufacture and application, as well as lacquers.

68. ROMA, C. B. *Termite Control for Home Owners.* Los Angeles, C. B. Roma Co. [1956]. 348 p. Illus.

69. SCHULZ, H. C. "The Care and Storage of Manuscripts in the Huntington Library." *Library Quarterly*, 5 (1935), 78-86.

70. SCRIBNER, B. W. "Preservation of Records in Libraries." *Library Quarterly*, 4 (1934), 371-83.

71. SCRIVEN, MARGARET. "Preservation and Restoration of Library Materials." *Special Libraries*, 47 (1956), 439-48. Illus. A description of practices at the Chicago Historical Society. As the author is aware, the cautious and conservative will raise an eyebrow at some of them: the use of wallpaper cleaner to remove dirt from documents, Permafilm (a transparent adhesive paper) for repair, and adhesive cloth for mounting maps.

72. SHAFFER, ELLEN. "Black Magic . . ." *Library Journal*, 84 (1959), 3832. Sulphur used in a cork composition lining an exhibition case gave off fumes which blackened a silver pigment in an early manuscript in the Free Library of Philadelphia. Also pointed out is the fact that electrostatic "air-purifiers" do not remove such fumes from the air.

73. SMITH, W. J. [Letter on silver fish]. *Antiquarian Bookman*, 24 (1959), 739. On the use of flour in jelly glasses at the University of Califorina at Los Angeles to trap silver fish.

74. STILL, J. S. "Library Fire and Salvage Methods." *American Archivist*, 16 (1953), 145-53.

75. TAUBER, MAURICE F., ED. "Conservation of Library Materials." *Library Trends*, 4 (1956), 213-334. Preservation as an administrative problem, discussed by a variety of contributors.

76. ———— *Technical Services in Libraries*. New York, Columbia University Press [1954]. xvi, 487 p. See Chapters 15-17, "Conservation of Library Materials."

77. TRIBOLET, H. W. "Binding and Related Problems." *American Archivist*, 16 (1953), 115-26.

78. TURNER, R. W. S. "To Repair or Despair?" *American Archivist,* 20 (1957), 319-34. On limitations of the lamination process as practiced at the National Archives, with rebuttal by J. L. Gear. See also Wilson and Forshee (81).

79. VEITCH, FLETCHER P., AND OTHERS. "Polluted Atmosphere a Factor in the Deterioration of Bookbinding Leather." *Journal of the American Leather Chemists' Association,* 21 (1926), 156-76. Illus.

80. WEISS, HARRY B., AND RALPH H. CARRUTHERS. *Insect Enemies of Books.* New York, New York Public Library, 1937. 63 p. Illus. Includes, pp. 19-63, "An Annotated Bibliography to 1935." Reprinted from the *Bulletin* of the New York Public Library. Generally considered the best nontechnical discussion of the subject.

81. WILSON, W. K., AND B. W. FORSHEE. *Preservation of Documents by Lamination.* Washington, D.C., U.S. National Bureau of Standards, 1959. 19 p. (The Bureau's Monograph No. 5.) A reappraisal of the lamination process using cellulose acetate foil, which in effect substantiates the claims made in its behalf.

INDEX

Numbers prefixed by "R" designate items in the List of References (pp. 101-13). Otherwise paging is indicated.

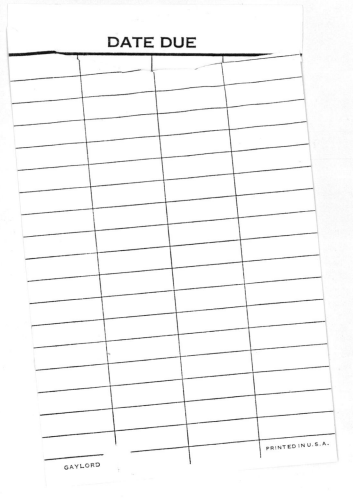

DATE DUE

GAYLORD

PRINTED IN U.S.A.